LEAD & MANAGE STRATEGICALLY

LEAD &
MANAGE
STRATEGICALLY

A SELF-GUIDED 6-STEP PROCESS FOR
ANY TYPE OR SIZE BUSINESS

JAMES R MOORE

XULON PRESS

Xulon Press
2301 Lucien Way #415
Maitland, FL 32751
407.339.4217
www.xulonpress.com

Printed in the United States of America.

Paperback ISBN-13: 978-1-6628-0231-7
eBook ISBN-13: 978-1-6628-0232-4

TABLE OF CONTENTS

ACKNOWLEDGEMENTS

I thank the whole host of clients over the 20 plus years of my consulting practice for their confidence in me as they embraced The Strategic Way Six-Step Process. They all had much greater success with their businesses as a result, but first had to have faith in my guidance as I walked them through the process.

A special thank you to the Director of the CompassCare Medical Services Center, Jim Harden, for his extraordinary embracement of the six-step process concepts from the beginning, which lead to the highest performing medical services center of this type in the USA.

And for the endurance of my wife, Carol, as I wrestled with the publication of this book.

Fourthly, to the publication team at XULON PRESS, a part of Salem Media Group, for their work in getting this book published.

And finally, to the Good Lord for giving me the concepts that I applied throughout the six-steps and the opportunity to apply them so successfully with so many businesses.

INTRODUCTION

This book is written to the leaders of businesses who are willing to take a portion of their precious time to read the book and apply the concepts presented in the six steps, in the hope of achieving the ideal vision for their businesses. In my experience as a manager in a major corporation, time is one of the most important assets to steward. The Six-Step Strategic Way Process addressed in this book is a tool to do just that and much, much more. When this process is implemented, everyone in the business knows the mission of the business, the ideal vision of the operation to carry out the vision and their role in achieving it.

Managers will have time to not only manage their portion of the day-to-day operation, but will have significant time to think about the future – to think strategically. This occurs because the day-to-day operation begins to run smoothly, under control and improving continuously.

Like the managers, individual contributors are able to carry out their roles with ever increasing excellence. As a result, they are a happier lot. Everybody in the business wins, even the suppliers to the business and most importantly, the receivers of the products and services.

Sound a bit utopian? Of course, because the operation is never perfect, but is ever improving at a rapid pace. Everyone in the business is constantly improving in carrying out their role with total awareness of their progress toward the ideal.

ABOUT THE AUTHOR

With a life time focus of wanting to make better whatever work I undertook, I saw the need to further my training when in my mid-twenties. I enrolled at the University of Wisconsin in a program that allowed me to major in applied math, electrical engineering and physics. Upon graduation, I went with a large corporation working on large aerospace systems, then shifted my focus to building totally automated manufacturing plants, again large systems.

When near the completion of updating a fourth plant, part of a separate business within the corporation, wherein, the business had lost money for ten years, I had an unexpected challenge. The new plant manager of this business was told to "Make a Buck" within the next year or the business would be shut down. The plant manager asked me what I would do to "Make a Buck". When my response was carried out, the business was making a buck in 9 months.

This launched my interest in optimizing management systems. For the remainder of my employment at the corporation, I lead a team that successfully trained eighty-one directors of research and engineering in twelve divisions of the corporation.

Taking an early retirement, I began consulting with all types and sizes of businesses with amazing results. I have authored this book to allow business leaders to get the same results I experienced as a consultant without my being present. What follows is the six-step process I have used, that you may now use, to optimize your management system and achieve the vision you have for your business.

Part I The Evolution: From Tactical to Strategic. Leaders spending an inordinate amount of their time focused on the day-to-day operation suggests a current situation that is tactical. Shifting their time to longer range issues, that is, strategic planning and implementation is where the majority of the leader's time should be focused. No one else will!

Chapter 1 The Business Vision: In the Hearts of the Leaders. The progress a business is making toward the vision the leaders have for their businesses is most often falling short of expectations. The leaders are working hard, giving every bit of thoughtful energy they can muster to move the business forward. In some situations, the business growth is flat or even losing ground. The current situation of most businesses is holding the leaders back from achieving their vision for the business. There is a solution to this dilemma.

Think of a business as a group of people organized to make their vision a reality.

The types of businesses I have helped include manufacturing, construction, professional services such as attorney firms, financial planners, marketing groups, medical service providers, nonprofits, even churches and educational institutions, just to name a few. The size of the organization has varied from a few people to a department, division or even a whole corporation.

Chapter 2 A Stake in the Ground: Leader's Commitment. It may be time leaders put a stake in the ground, that is, spending the time to walk through the Strategic Way Six-Step Process. Doing so, they will develop a strategic plan and, most importantly, the plan's implementation.

Chapter 3 The Launch. To set up for success, there are some preliminary steps that need to be taken. A development team, referred to as the Core Team, to carry out the first 3 steps, needs to be formed. A facilitator be positioned to guide the team through these steps. A resource group identified who may have a special knowledge or insight into the subjects addressed in these six steps. And the Core Team's commitment to meet weekly until the six steps are carried out.

Part II The Process: The Strategic Way Six-Steps. Leaders do have a vision for their businesses. For some it is crystal clear. For others it is broad, like a framework that needs to be filled in. For many, the progress toward the vision is not satisfactory. For others, there are roadblocks on this journey that are holding them back. The Strategic Way Process guides the development of a strategic plan. It then guides the removal of the major roadblocks to implementation. It evolves the business's current management system into one that is functioning strategically. The business is now on the way to achieving its vision to the satisfaction of the leaders and the whole workforce. Client stories of applying the process are presented throughout the book to demonstrate the effectiveness of the Strategic Way Process.

Chapter 4 Step 1–Strategically Driven: Where to, How to and Progress Along the Way. The objective of this step is to guide the Core Team in the process to develop the content of each element of the strategic plan which will be unique to their business. The strategic plan is the lynchpin around which the business succeeds in achieving the vision of the leaders and the hope of those having vested interests in the business: the employees, those who own the business, and of course, the recipients of its products and services.

Chapter 5 Step 2–Optimally Structured: A streamlined Workflow. The objective of this step is to optimize the organization structure for the implementation of the newly developed strategic plan. The existing structure is often less than optimal. The structure has most likely evolved over time as the business changed due to innovation in the operation, changing technology, changes to the products and services, changes in leadership as well as other issues.

Chapter 6 Step 3–Career Matched: Right People in the Right Positions. With the business level strategic plan developed and the organization structure optimized to best support implementing the strategic plan, the objective of this step is to put people in positions that best serve them in their career plans and best serve the business in carrying out its mission and achieving its vision.

Chapter 7 Step 4–Strategically Implemented: Closer to the production floor. The Core Team has completed the business strategic plan, optimized the organization structure and has now matched people to the work at business level. It is time to shift focus from business level to next level down in the organization structure referred to as the Key Result Areas (KRA's). What key part do each of these areas play strategically in the business? The objective of this step is to develop strategic plans for each area guided by the business strategic plan.

Chapter 8 Step 5–Team Operated: Teams of Teams. The objective of step 5 is to define the operation management approach that will implement the business level strategic plan. Breaking down the tasks within the KRA's to most effectively carry out the work is critical to the implementation of each area strategic plan. In a very real sense, it is time to take the plan to the work floor, into the task by task action required to carry out the strategic plan at area level.

Chapter 9 Step 6–Progress Managed: Achieving Operations Excellence. The objective of this step is to bring both the management and work floor work processes to excellence and continually improve them, fundamental to a healthy business. Excellence manifests itself in products and services that consistently meet the needs of the user and require a minimum period of time and resources to produce.

Part III: Toward the Destination: About Leadership. Over a couple of decades of working with a wide spectrum of businesses one cannot help but gain some insight into leadership. As you may have observed by now, I am interested in results, not theories or generalizations about what sounds like it would be effective. My interest is in positive results that I have observed about management that I have concluded are generally applicable in most businesses. The objective of Part III is to share a collection of such observations to which I have been exposed, recurring over time, in a variety of environments.

Chapter 10: Effective Leadership: Expecting results. There are some proven, effective, and straightforward ways leaders can gain the understanding and engagement of the workforce. With significant changes in the business operation taking place as the steps of The Strategic Way Process are carried out, to be fruitful, the workforce needs to be made aware of and allowed to participate in a manner that is orderly and timely. Celebrations, rollouts, and organized communications will certainly make the work of the leadership far more effective.

Chapter 11 Celebrations: Real Need–Small cost. Imagine a business where co-workers recognize when someone accomplishes something of value and gives the person a compliment, round of applause, slap on the back or words such as *good job, way to go, great effort.* Then take it a step further and see little celebrations of coffee and pastries or hand out of a certificate of appreciation made up on a personal computer. And on occasion where the initiative is taken to invite an individual or team out for lunch or provide tickets to some special event. Where there is an atmosphere where people are trying to catch associates doing something right and letting them know that their efforts are appreciated. This is characteristic of a healthy business. The objective of this chapter is to share how to create this atmosphere throughout your business.

Chapter 12 Reflections: The Experience. The Strategic Way Process addresses major issues every business operation encounters. For any one business, there may be only a few issues that need attention. If the business is satisfactorily carrying out its mission and moving at an acceptable pace toward its vision than this process could be viewed as an audit. If all the stakeholders are satisfied with the performance of the business than the only concern would be to maintain or exceed that level of performance. This reference to stakeholders includes the receivers of the products and services, people that produce them, the governance of the business and the owners.

Appendix A: Glossary of Terms. Reference to the Glossary of Terms seeks to maintain a common language throughout the business workforce regarding the management system developed and the business operation. It is important that the whole workforce is using a common language.

Appendix B: The Strategic Way Six- Step Tasks: The tasks that follow, guide the facilitator in walking through each of the 6 steps.

Appendix C: The Strategic Way Rollout. When a team has completed work that needs to be understood, enhanced, owned, accepted by and complied with by a group of people, an effective process to accomplish this is a Strategic Way Rollout which will be referred to simply as a Rollout.

Appendix D: Insights toward more effective leadership. I am noting insights made in my years of experience as a manager and as a management consultant.

THE EVOLUTION

From Tactical to Strategic

Business leaders are challenged to produce products and services that meet the needs of their targeted market. They seek to grow a business which consistently serves the needs of the market place while providing employment for the whole workforce, a reasonable return to the investors and hopefully, a better community for all to live within. Most business leaders would agree with these objectives and yet, most are not satisfied with the progress of their businesses toward meeting these objectives.

THE BUSINESS VISION

In the Hearts of Leaders

Poke at leaders enough and they will tell you the vision they have for the business they lead. They may do this with some reluctance for not being sure of how it will be received. Or they may have thought out the vision only in broad terms. Their vision may be a framework that needs to be filled in, putting meat on the bones, so to speak. It may take the combined contribution of several or all of the leaders to fully describe the vision of the ideal future state of their business. But one thing is sure, leaders have a vision for their business somewhere in their thinking.

For the sake of simplicity, I refer to all types of organizations as businesses.

Think of a business as a group of people organized to make their vision a reality.

These businesses include manufacturing, construction, professional services such as attorney firms, financial planners, marketing groups, medical service providers, non-profits, even churches and educational institutions, just to name a few.

The size of the organization could be a few people or a department, division or a whole corporation. Government agencies are equally fair game. The concepts presented here can be applied to a small business that has one, two, three or more levels of management. It can and has been applied within a large corporation that had 7 levels of management. It has been applied to a 46-million-dollar program involving the Massachusetts Institute of Technology and eleven prominent large corporations. The concepts apply regardless of the organization type and size.

THE BUSINESS LEADER'S DILEMMA
The Current Situation

The progress a business is making toward the vision the leaders have for the business is most often falling short of expectations. These leaders are most often working hard, giving every bit of thoughtful energy they can muster to move the business forward. In some situations, the business growth is flat or even losing ground.

Not only the leaders, but the whole workforce is sensing this business condition. How could they not. They are there every day working hard, sensing the lack of progress toward what may be a somewhat unclear vision the leaders have of where they want the business to go. Often the workforce is convinced that this uncertain state of the business will never change.

This lack of clear vision and progress toward it is wide spread in businesses across the land.

A significant percentage of leaders don't really know how to improve the state of their business. Although many will have sought out help from leaders of other more successful businesses, have attended seminars, hired consultants, have sought online research or pursued more formal education. All too often not getting the desired help they need. There certainly must be a way to clarify the vision for the business and the means to achieve it.

Presented throughout this book as client stories are the results of using a six-step process I developed, The Strategic Way Process, which I have used in a wide array of businesses. The businesses are distinctly different in type and size. The stories give a realistic sense of the profound improvement realized when the Strategic Way Process is applied.

The names of the businesses and associated leaders in the stories have been changed but the transformations occurred just as described.

These business leaders carrying out the steps of the Strategic Way Process have experienced dramatic improvement in otherwise less than acceptable operation performance. All businesses described lacked a strategic plan although some had a three or five-year plan. These operations had one or more roadblocks on the journey to achieving the vision the leaders had for their businesses.

In every endeavor, what is intended to be accomplished is not always apparent but is critical to be agreed upon by the leadership and understood and supported by the whole workforce in order to establish unity and effectiveness of operation.

ISSUES BUSINESS LEADERS FACE
Roadblocks to the vision

A business should be traveling down the road toward the collective vision of its leaders. If the vision were clearly expressed and communicated, there should be clear signs that the business is approaching the desired vision. And yet often that is not what the leaders are experiencing. Then what are the road blocks to achieving their vision?

Let's examine the way leaders of these businesses often do their planning. Most have an annual plan. The plan includes a somewhat limited set of measures used to determine progress of the business. Goals are set based upon these measures and some rationale or set of approaches for meeting them often referred to as strategies.

The measures typically include the quantity of products and services to be delivered, share of the market if that is relevant, quality of the products and services they are or plan to produce, budgeting of costs and acceptable profit goals. This is likely to be familiar to anyone in any form of business. Even non-profits want to break even regarding costs versus income. Annual plans often have little reference to long range thinking that could be built into the planning process.

The approach (strategy) for meeting these goals is often discussed but may not be documented. Lack of documentation assumes that all have memories that don't lapse when in the heat of carrying out the day-to-day operations. The approaches may not be communicated to the whole workforce. It should not be surprising then, that these approaches are not consistently carried out throughout the workforce. They may not be aware or don't know how the approaches translate down to their level.

Many times, the people on the floor transforming client needs into products and services are not kept abreast of progress toward these goals. For them it is like playing in a football game without a scoreboard. Throughout the year and at year end the progress toward the achievement of the goals or lack thereof may or may not be communicated to the workers. If that is so, then it would not be surprising that the workers would not be inspired during the year to work more effectively or even to know when they are being effective. They may not know the score and at year end not know if the goals were met, that is, did we win!

They not only are uninspired about their work but are not influenced to make relevant strategic decisions as they perform their work, that is, as they play the game. As the performance of the players in the football game are influenced by their awareness of the yards to go to make a first down or the effect of scoring to win the game, so too would the workers on the floor be positively influenced if they only knew how close they were to meeting the goals.

Aside from planning and progress awareness, many times the tyranny of the urgent keeps the leaders focused on the short term. The urgent issues that face many managers daily may take the form of one or more of the following: Operations under their responsibility have personnel issues that keep popping up; unpredictable or underperforming work processes creating reoccurring issues; an unacceptable percent of customers or clients of the products and services are complaining, suppliers are grumbling and the list goes on and on.

The managers are having to deal with these issues as well as having to plow daily through email and paperwork. There are a multitude of interruptions with phone calls and office drop-ins. Much of their time may be spent in meetings solving tactical problems or answering to those to whom they are accountable. Is it any wonder these managers don't spend much time planning for the long term or significantly improving the management system within which they operate. They just work to keep their heads above water handling the day-to-day issues.

Even if they could carve out some time to create and implement strategic plans, they likely do not have the experience or knowledge to effectively create these plans and gain the support of their workforce. Creating the content of these plans would be enough of a challenge. There are straightforward processes to create the strategic plans but the leaders are unaware of them. Good news! Herein is the process to create these plans—Chapter 4 Step 1 Strategically Driven.

And then there is the issue of modifying their business's management system sufficiently to implement the plans. Every business has a system of managing the work, that is, how things get done, from budgeting to writing sales orders and subsequent work orders, to biding new business, to guiding the engagement of their clients, to seeing patients, etc. It all depends on the type of business and the evolution of the system. Their current management system has probably evolved out of the thinking of past managers. Little if any effort may have been made to improve the current management system, often because this is foreign territory for them.

What about the person holding a key position that is not only not effectively carrying out his or her responsibilities but actually seems uncomfortable in the position. Most everyone has observed this situation at some time in their career, but the person continues in the role. This occurs far more often than not in businesses for profit or not. The issue continues with the operation's effectiveness affected in a most negative way.

This situation is demoralizing to the workforce as it has a negative effect on the productivity of the operation. Let us not ignore the effect on the individuals that come to work knowing their shortcomings for the positions they fill. The issue typically goes unresolved because those in authority to act do not have awareness of how to address it without leaving a trail of blood on the field.

Consider the allocation of human resources. Are the right people in the key positions within the organization structure? What is best for the operation of the business and best for their career development. One would certainly hope so. Too often this is not the case. Wouldn't it be great if there was a process that could be used on a regular basis to address this issue? There is! Read on.

When the subject is brought up of using teams to carry out the functions of the operation there are these typical responses from leaders. We've tried using teams. It doesn't work in our business. Teams are difficult to manage as they go out of control becoming islands unto themselves. We have difficulty developing team people strong enough and in sufficient numbers to lead the teams. Trust me, these issues can be addressed effectively.

And then there is this whole thing of defining, documenting and consistently using and bringing to excellence the operation's management and work processes. In some operations, time may be taken to identify and document these processes. Even if done, the documentation becomes out of date. The work processes are often written in narrative form resulting in difficulty to use and update when necessary. When this occurs, the documentation is then not followed. The processes are then carried out inconsistently. And yet a lack of good documentation to manage the processes is a barrier to the pursuit of excellence throughout the operation.

The issues reviewed here are symptoms of management systems that need development into a better state. What an effectively evolved management system would look like is the next topic. Business leaders can evolve their current business management system into ones that resolves the above noted issues and yet retain the esoteric and essential elements of the current management system.

A MANAGEMENT SYSTEM TO LEAD STRATEGICALLY
Issues Resolved

Development of a Strategically Optimized Management System (SOMS) addresses and resolves the issues leaders face that keep them and the workforce they lead from achieving the vision they have for their businesses. The unique SOMS is developed by walking through the Six-Step Strategic Way Process for the business.

The SOMS captures the leader's vision and then drives it across every area of the organization structure. This includes down to the production floor where people transform client needs into the products and services the business produces.

When everyone in the operation is cognizant of where the business is intended to go, that is, the destination, the mission and ideal vision of the operation, how it plans to get there and actually see progress toward that destination, there is a profound unity that comes over the workforce. From the managers to the individual contributors there is an obvious pulling together of all involved. Each seeking to add value to the extent possible in their role.

Businesses have these characteristics that evolve from however the operations were managed to a SOMS system.

- The whole workforce knows the planned destination of the business.
- Everyone is adding value to get there to the level of their ability.
- There are clear data tracking the progress and influencing every decision made by the leaders and every worker down to the production floor.

- And they all know the progress being made toward achieving the business vision.
- The business is structured organizationally to optimize the effectiveness of carrying out the operation functions.
- The right people are in the right positions to carry out the functions for which they are responsible. T whole workforce to actively and deliberately pursue their career goals.
- The business level strategic plan is translated down to the level of the key result areas of the operation.
- Teams are functioning at all levels of the organization structure to most effectively carry out all of the operation functions.
- All of the teams have documented processes that are followed and continuously improved as the processes move toward excellence.
- Managers at all levels are spending more than half their time quietly working in their offices or work stations.

Where the tyranny of the urgent is a thing of the past.

The SOMS becomes the vehicle to guide the business operation down the road to achieve the vision the whole workforce is now seeking to achieve.

This transition to a SOMS occurs over several years.

When using the Six-Step Strategic Way Process is applied, the greatest changes occur in the first year. In the following years, there are continual annual adjustments as the business environment changes and new insights are learned. The transition requires thoughtful work being done by all.

As the transition begins there typically is a great deal of hope and anticipation expressed by the leaders and the whole workforce. All are encouraged as this journey progresses toward the vision, the destination of the business.

TRANSITION TO A STRATEGICALLY OPTIMIZED MANAGEMENT SYSTEM
The Strategic Way Process

Commonly occurring management issues can be resolved by the current leadership with the support of the whole workforce.

With the guidance of the six-step Strategic Way Process, the leadership of a business can evolve its operation into a Strategically Optimized Management System (SOMS). It addresses all of the above described issues and more.

It does not resolve a poorly thought out business plan. If you do not produce products and services that are meeting the needs of the market you are targeting, little can be done to the management system to improve it other than modify the business plan.

Most likely you have products and services that are needed in the market place. Your operation is just not managed as well as it needs to be to effectively deliver them.

Any management system can be evolved to function as a SOMS. The obvious question then is how do leaders achieve this transition? It may be a tweaking of the current system or possibly a major shift from their current system of management?

A well proven process for making this shift is the Strategic Way Process. This process has six steps that transforms a current business management system into one that exhibits the characteristics of a SOMS™ . It builds the vehicle, the SOMS, to move the operation down the road toward the vision the leaders have envisioned for the business. This SOMS is a vehicle unique to that business. The Strategic Way Process is the method the leaders of that business will use to build their vehicle. The process accomplishes this transition just as well with all types of businesses.

As noted earlier, this process does not produce an overnight transition to the SOMS. It occurs over time with the Strategic Way Process being applied annually. Each run through the process steps moves the business's management system closer and closer to the ideal for that particular business. The first time through the process requires the greatest amount of time and produces the greatest change to the current management system.

EVOLUTION OF YOUR MANAGEMENT SYSTEM
What to expect

When used annually, the six steps of the Strategic Way Process evolve the current business management system into a far more effective system, the Strategically Optimized Management System (SOMS). Many, if not all of the participants in pursuing the 6-step process are traveling down a road that is new to them. Work is being done on the first journey that will require much less time in future trips through the 6-step process.

There are valid and relevant questions that need to be answered before the leaders of a business should consider making the transition.

Does using the Strategic Way Process require expertise beyond the leadership of the business?
Not at all! Using Chapter 3–The Launch will guide the business leaders in the required preparation to carry out the 6-step process. Chapters 4 through 9 are specifically designed to guide the leaders through the 6 steps of the Strategic Way Process™.

Does it totally disrupt the daily operation of the business?
No! It requires one two-hour session per week in a meeting with three to eight attenders. Two sessions can be held each week to speed up the process but is not required. At least one session per week is needed to maintain continuity of thought.

Can only certain types of businesses succeed at making this transformation?
Haven't found one yet that couldn't successfully transition to a unique SOMS for their business.

How long will it take to achieve this transformation?

The first time through the six-step process takes by far the longest. How long depends on the current thinking of the business leadership regarding the topics covered. For example: Is there an existing mission statement? Has the leadership given recent thought to the vision for the business? Some leaders may be able to glide through some steps relatively quickly while others may take significant time. The longer it takes to get through a step suggests the more value the step adds to that business. With each time through the 6-step process in the following years there is typically little to be done with mission and vision statements and values. Most of the new work each year is updating the current situation, modifying the strategies based on changes in the business environment and evolving development through the remaining 5 steps.

What should leaders expect from using the Strategic Way Process™?

Some new management concepts may be introduced of which the managers were just not previously aware. In other cases, they may not know how to make the changes they know are needed. A common occurrence is in the application of the continuous improvement cycle and other Total Quality Management concepts presented in step 6. As much as these concepts have been mentioned in business circles over the years, many leaders do not understand them or know how to implement them. Some but certainly not all quality concepts will be introduced in step 6. As the positive results of these concepts being applied are realized there will undoubtedly be a desire to pursue other Total Quality Management concepts outside of what is presented in step 6.

Another area of change may occur when self-managed teams are introduced. Properly done, this can make a profound improvement in the operation. When effectively implemented there is a shift of responsibility to the lowest level with appropriate guidance and accountability put in place. All will benefit as the people at lower levels are able to assume more responsibility making their roles richer in content and simultaneously at higher levels the managers are free to focus on broader issues.

The steps can be applied with equally effective results to any and all businesses whose leaders are seeking to offer the very best in products and services to their customers and clients. This includes nonprofit businesses that may not think of themselves delivering products and services, but I would suggest that they are doing exactly that. When people are organized to accomplish something, whether products, services or influence of the environment within or around them, the SOMS will have a significantly positive impact on their visions being achieved.

TACTICAL TO STRATEGIC MANAGEMENT
An Amazing Shift

Top down strategic planning keeps the leader's focus on the long-term business target or destination. Annually going through refinement of the strategic plan keeps managers conscious of the long term when making annual or short term plans. Because the 6-step process engages the whole workforce at several points, all within the business have this same consciousness of the long-term direction. In this work there is also the assurance that some part of the strategies may need to be kept to only those in the business who have a need to know. That condition should always be honored.

It often surprises leaders with how much the business benefits from the whole workforce being engaged in understanding and even enhancing the plans. This is done through The Strategic Way Process Rollouts (which will be referred to simply as rollouts). Through rollouts of the first three steps of the process the workforce naturally transitions to not only understanding the plans, the structure changes and the positioning of people, but really owns these changes to the business operation, a manager's dreams come true. I have seen this transition occur over and over in a wide spectrum of businesses. Coming to work becomes more and more enjoyable for not only the managers but the production floor workers as well and every one in between. It is wonderful to experience.

THE OUTCOME
Everybody Wins

The leaders at all levels are ensuring that feedback on performance is occurring within the system at every level. Goals are being set that are stretch and yet attainable, with plans being executed to close the gap between the baseline and the goals. Goals are set at the top but negotiated down through the organization to ensure they are attainable.

At all levels, from the business leaders to the process operators on the work floor, everyone has understanding and control over what they are to be doing, how and why it is to be done, and its importance at each level.

Is this not what is desired in any business? An important outcome of this effort is that people are likely to be working to their level of capability and growing in capability over time. Products and services should thus be serving the recipients in ways not previously achieved. Owners are reaping returns on the funds they have invested and have reason to believe the return on investment will increase over time.

The Strategic Way Process couples the concepts of strategic planning with the steps necessary for successful implementation. The process challenges leaders of all types of businesses: small and medium size businesses, large corporations and their divisions, physician groups, educational institutions, government entities and non-profits.

In all of these business settings it is the leader's responsibility to set a clear destination and the means of reaching it. No one else has this role. If the leaders don't take on the role, confusion and frustration prevail. The Strategic Way Process demonstrates how leaders, with some guidance from this book coupled with a skilled facilitator and the willingness to change, can set a clear direction, remove roadblocks and engage the total workforce in carrying out the mission and achieving the vision of their businesses.

A STAKE IN THE GROUND

Leader's Commitment

P icture leaders seeking to achieve the vision for their business, wanting to experience the growth that has been sought for years. Perhaps just stability would be a good start, or possibly reversing a business decline that has been occurring over a period of time.

The client stories provided word pictures of the way many issues impeding progress were resolved by employing the Strategic Way Process™. Is it possible that your business can be helped in a similar way, perhaps not with the exact same issues but issues that are keeping your business from achieving the vision you have sought?

The Strategic Way Process does not directly address the business plan, find investment capital, research needed technology, etc., but it does walk you through the fundamentals of organization development that evolve the current management system into a Strategically Driven Management System™. The whole workforce is now focused on the destination, your clearly stated mission you need to carry out and your carefully documented inspiring vision you desire to achieve.

It may be time to put the proverbial stake in the ground and address your issues head-on. The workers on the floor won't do it. The people who fund your business won't do it. The recipients of your business's products and services won't do it. Your suppliers won't do it. They all wish somebody would. Who then, but you?

When that first step of the Strategic Way Process is completed creating the business strategic plan and rolled out to the total workforce, typically there is true awe expressed. There is that sense amongst the people that things that needed to change heretofore were thought to be forever unchanging, are being changed. When the organization structure is optimized, the right people are matched to the right positions and so on through the process, the workers now know the leaders are serious about moving the business forward. This is not the "Program of the Month." It is not a rifle shot that is supposed to solve every issue. It is the result of sometimes difficult, always thoughtful work, to turn the business in a direction in which all will benefit.

A stake in the ground here means to commit to embracing the total process. The Strategic Way Process is a series of 6 steps, a linear process which, to be most effective, must involve all 6 steps carried out in order. Cherry-picking any fewer than the 6 may well leave a roadblock that would greatly inhibit the success of the business. Commit to the whole 6 step process for as long as it takes. With each step, significant progress will be made.

Chapters 4 through 9 attempt to make the 6-step process as concise as possible and yet convey the essentials of working through each step. Equally important is to have a skilled facilitator in place to guide the process. As leaders, you need to focus on the content each step is designed to produce. If a large business, there are surely people who can fill the facilitator role. In a nonprofit, you will probably need to find someone floating around in your volunteer base who could carry out this role. For any size business, a facilitator is essential. The facilitator guides the process using the tasks in Appendix B.

When the leaders at the top are convinced there is the need and they are humble enough to admit it, it is time to put a stake in the ground and commit to embracing the Strategic Way Process whole- heartedly. Success will hinge on the leaders' commitment to carry the 6 steps all the way through. It will require a minimum of one two-hour meeting a week, perhaps speeding up the process with two meetings per week, of five to eight top leaders to form a Core Team that will drive the walk through the first three of the 6 process steps. This represents 5 to 10% of the Core Team's work week for a significant period of time.

This requires the leaders to stop throwing all their resources at the tyranny of the urgent and allocate appropriate resources to provide long-term solutions and significantly reduce the urgent, hopefully eliminating most or all of this day to day stuff that can consume far too much of their time.

The intent, at all levels of the business, from the highest level of management to the work floor, should be to get the processes that carry out the functions under control and brought to excellence. Everyone, especially the leaders, will then have some time to reflect on the longer-term issues of the business.

I have provided for your awareness and encouragement true stories of what has been accomplished by a wide spectrum of businesses using the 6-step process. For some leaders there has been presented enough of a description of the application of the concepts and the results obtained that they will readily launch into the 6-step process.

For others, more information about the 6 steps will be needed to make a decision. They may need to read Chapters 4 through 9 to gain the understanding needed to decide. That is fine too. Chapter 3 The Launch, will guide them through preparation for walking through the 6 steps. For some, all that has been presented may need to incubate for a time. Then they may choose to go through the 6 steps. That may be necessary to make the commitment of time to work through the 6 steps. And for some it is just not judged to be for their business.

I wish business leaders well making any one of these decisions. It is your business, your resources and your responsibility to lead your business. The next step is up to you. I sincerely wish you great success in your journey to carry out the mission and achieve the vision of your business.

CHAPTER

3

THE LAUNCH

Now to Set Up for Success

To set in motion the Strategic Way Process, I suggest having current leaders of the business read Chapters 4 through 9 describing the 6 steps to determine if they are willing to commit the resources to carrying out The Six-Step Strategic Way Process.

If yes, then those leaders willing to form the Core Team (3 to 8 members) need to commit to spend the time needed to carry out the first three steps. To be most effective.to the time required in the first run through steps 1-3 is typically two hours per week until these steps are completed.

Lower level managers will carry out step 4 and 5. All members of the workforce will engage in continuous improvement covered in step 6.

FORM THE CORE TEAM
This team will carry out the first 3 steps

I have never observed a reluctance for some leaders to partici-pate in this development work once the leadership gets even the briefest description of what will be accomplished. A great way to inspire up and coming leaders is to engage one or more of them in this work as well. Some current managers may support this work but do not have an interest in doing the development work or do not have the time to do so. Where that is the case, assure these managers that they will have ample opportunity to influence the work done in the first 3 steps without having to be on the devel-opment team.

Call the group selected to do this development work, the Core Team. Depending on the size of the business the team may include as few as 3 members or as many as 8. More than 8 really bogs down the progress forward through the steps. With fewer than 3 there is a lack of richness of experience and thinking from which to draw.

Where ever in the business this process is being applied, the team membership should include the business's manager at that level. This may be the owner if a small business, a division director if a large business or the CEO of a corporation. The process has worked well at the top level of a corporation as well as deep within the organization structure.

The Core Team's role is to think through and document a draft of the content generated in the first 3 steps of the process: the business strategic plan, the optimized organization structure and matching of career plans to organization level positions. The Core Team must make a high-level time commitment to see these 3 steps through to completion.

Schedule one meeting a week of the Core Team on Tuesday, Wednesday or Thursday. The first day of the work week is involved in ramping up normal operation activities for the week. The last day of the work week has worn the participants down to where they are not at their best. Two hour weekly sessions will achieve great productivity. Meeting weekly assures a level of continuity in thinking yet minimizes the time taken from the week's daily work.

Keep in mind that the Core Team meetings are not about resolving day-to-day issues but about developing a Strategically Optimized Management System, a major investment in the future of the business. Allow no interruptions to the sessions. Need I suggest that cell phones be turned off. Stiff the tyrant of the urgent. If someone must miss a meeting leave open the opportunity for that person to provide input at the next meeting. To maintain continuity this must not occur often.

ENGAGE A FACILITATOR
Guides the process–Replaces the consultant

I strongly suggest a facilitator be brought in to guide the Core Team through each step. My role as consultant was to facilitate the 6-step process. The facilitator will be replacing me as the consultant. I purposely avoided contributing content unless it was very obvious that it would help them think through their work. These leaders on the Core Team need to wrestle with, take ownership of and be accountable for the content resulting from working through the first 3 steps. I have found that it is not practical for these leaders to play the dual role of content providers and facilitator.

Typically, someone in the business has facilitation skills. Appendix B: The Strategic Way 6 Tasks, is intended to be used by the facilitator to guide the Core Team in the first three steps and then the KRA teams through the last three steps. The facilitator should not typically contribute content but keep the group focused on the task at hand. If a facilitator internal to the business is not available, it is worthwhile to bring one in from outside of the business. Facilitators best carry out their role if they study Chapters 4 through 9 and then follow the tasks described in Appendix B. The Core Team should read the book before the first meeting and reference Chapters 4 through 6 throughout the series of meetings.

IDENTIFY THE RESOURCE GROUP
The wise man seeks the counsel of many

It has proven valuable to identify a second group referred to as the Resource Group consisting of 5 or more people that may come from within or outside of the business. They may be identified as the Strategic Way Process steps are carried out. These people may have a special knowledge or insight into the subject at hand in one or more of the process steps. They typically come for 1 or 2 meetings to share their thinking and then are respectfully thanked and dismissed. They may be called in at a later time to provide insight into a subsequent process step.

Keep in mind that at the end of the first step, Strategically Driven, the work done to date by the Core Team will be rolled out to the business leaders who are not a part of the Core Team and then to the whole workforce and to the governing body members if that is appropriate. The rollout process is described in chapter 4 and Appendix C. When the rollout occurs eyes will open. The presentation will build great excitement and encouragement that the leaders are dead serious about moving the business forward. Most in the audience will not have seen this kind of business management system development before. It is typically a real breath of fresh air.

At the end of the third step a second rollout will take place. At this time any changes to the organization structure and role assignments will be reviewed. In both rollouts the audience will be asked to affirm what they like about the Core Team work and how they would enhance it. All responses are to be considered by the Core Team and incorporated only as the team deems appropriate. Engaging everyone in the process builds understanding and ownership within the workforce at all levels. I have seen this positive response over and over again.

CREATE A FORUM TO ADDRESS THE FUTURE
Commit the time and resources

To achieve the results so many other businesses have realized, launch into the Strategic Way Process with commitment to the time, thought and perseverance necessary to modify the existing management system into a Strategically Optimized Management System. This will remove the roadblocks so that you can effectively make progress toward the business vision. As the leadership, you are in complete control of what is changed. You will have gotten affirmation and suggested changes from all in leadership and from the whole workforce before any changes are actually put in place.

As you work through the Strategic Way Process you have the forum to address:

- A strategic plan: Clarification of the desired future state of the business, how to get to that future state and the means to measure progress along the way
- The optimal organization structure to carry out the plan
- Placement of the right people in the right positions in the organization structure
- Propagating of the strategic plan down to the key result areas of the operation
- Establishment of a team approach to management and operation of the business
- Implementation of concepts to achieve excellence in all of the business processes–management and work-floor processes.

Lack of a forum to address these issues has kept many business leaders from taking action.

Committing to completing the 6 steps of the Strategic Way Process™, creates a forum to address the future

Chapters 4 through 9 describe the *6 steps of the Strategic Way Process* in enough detail for the Core Team, made up of business leaders and a facilitator, to develop the strategic plan, optimize the organization structure and match the right people to the right positions. The facilitator will use a set of guidelines in Appendix B to draw out the content from the Core Team members and from individuals identified in the Resource Group.

At the appropriate time the work of the Core Team will be rolled out to all the leadership and ultimately to the whole workforce. In the roll out the work done will be presented with 2 questions asked of the audience: 1) What did you like about the results of the Core Team work presented? 2) How could the work be enhanced? The responses will be taken back for assessment by the Core Team.

This roll out process engages all the leaders and ultimately the whole workforce. In this process everyone is engaged, gaining a much stronger sense of ownership in the business and the direction it is headed. A profound unity is established within the workforce which leads to a more effective operation and workplace environment.

PART II

THE PROCESS

The Strategic Way Six Steps

Leaders do have a vision for their businesses. For some it is crystal clear. For others it is broad, like a framework that needs to be filled in. For many the progress toward the vision is not satisfactory. For others there are roadblocks on this journey that are holding back the business. The Strategic Way Process has been briefly described in the introduction. This process guides the development of a strategic plan. It then guides the removal of major roadblocks in its implementation. It evolves the business's current management system into one that is functioning strategically. The business is now on the way to achieving its vision to the satisfaction of the leaders and the whole workforce.

Client stories of applying the process have been presented demonstrating the effectiveness of the Strategic Way Process™ . The characteristics of a Strategically Optimized Management System™ , the result of using the Strategic Way Process™ , have been reviewed. A description of the transition from the current management system of a business to a Strategically Optimized Management System was presented. Expectations of applying the process were given.

It is time to describe the Strategic Way Process in sufficient detail to guide the leadership of any type or size of business in carrying out the process. When the 6 steps of the process are completed the leaders can reap the harvest of evolving toward a Strategically Optimized Management System™ .

STEP 1-STRATEGICALLY DRIVEN

Where to, How to and Progress Along the Way

The Strategic Way Process Steps:
> ***Strategically Driven–You are here***
> Optimally Structured
> Career Matched
> Strategically Implemented
> Team Operated
> Progress Managed

The objective of this chapter is to guide the Core Team in developing the content of each element of the strategic plan which will be unique to their business. The Core Team should read this chapter just prior to carrying out this step. The team will be guided through this first step of the Strategic Way Process by the team facilitator. The facilitator will read this chapter to anticipate the kind of content expected from the Core Team. The facilitator will use the Strategic Way Process documentation in Appendix B to guide the team as they generate the content. The leaders will focus on strategic plan content. The facilitator will focus on guiding the team through the process. Very different roles.

The strategic plan is the lynchpin around which the business succeeds in achieving the vision of the leaders and the hope of those having vested interests in the business; the employees, those who own the business, and of course, the recipients of the products and services.

When the workforce shifts from focusing on the problems of the moment to directing all resources at all times toward a commonly viewed destination the business operation is becoming strategically driven.

THE ELEMENTS OF A STRATEGIC PLAN
The long-range thinking that guides the whole workforce.

The business strategic plan addresses three major questions. These three fundamental questions will be answered by the Core Team as its members are prompted by a breakdown of these questions.

1. Where are we going?
   a. Where are we now–The current situation?
   b. What is our work, who is it directed at and why do this work–The mission?
   c. What are the outcomes of doing the work–The evidence of carrying out the mission?
   d. Ideally what does the operation look like–The Vision?
   e. The combination of carrying out the mission and achieving the vision represents the destination–The business target.

2. How will we get there?
   a. What values must we embrace which will change the culture so that we can reach the destination?
   b. What are the current strategies?
   c. What are the enhanced or newly developed strategies we must implement?

3. How will we measure progress along the way?
   a. The currently used measures?
   b. The enhanced or newly defined measure?

ASSESSING THE CURRENT SITUATION
A snapshot of today's operation

Documenting the current situation is the starting point on the journey toward the mission and vision that will soon be developed. The current situation describes where the business is now; it also weaves in a bit of history. The main thrust is to clarify the business's strengths, identify weaknesses that need to be turned into strengths and to identify opportunities for and threats to the business. This focus on Strengths, Weaknesses, Opportunities and Threats is commonly referred to as a SWOT analysis.

The Core Team, the leaders, and ultimately the whole workforce need to become conscious of where the business is at present. The current situation describes the firm base that the business has hopefully established and at the same time recognizes a need to move forward toward a much better future state.

The history relates to how the business got to where it is now. It will be difficult to do so, but it is necessary to keep it brief. It is most important for the leaders to make clear where the business is now. Thinking through the reality of the current situation is key to successfully setting a direction for the future state.

Strategic planning is not about looking back over one's shoulder, but rather looking forward toward the horizon and beyond.

An effective means of documenting the current situation is to look inward. To address the strengths and weaknesses of the business and recognize what has to be strengthened. Knowing where the business is strong will reinforce a competitive edge when defining the mission. It will be important to maintain these existing strengths. Recognition of where weaknesses appear sets in motion thoughts of strategies for strengthening these areas. The objective is to be strong in whatever areas the business needs to be strong to carry out the mission successfully.

With the Core Team having identified the strengths and the weaknesses that need to be turned into strengths, this process is used to look outward beyond the business into the market place for opportunities. This will help clarify where the leaders intend to direct the products and services, that is, what markets to target. Knowing the threats in the marketplace is equally important. Knowing what could keep the business from being successful allows thinking through a mission and strategies to avoid or minimize the threats.

There are normally people on the Core Team who know the history of the business. If not, seek these insights from the Resource Group. Throughout this process it may be useful to tap the Resource Group for help. It may also be necessary to retain a consultant with expertise in this industry or business to critique the current operation and make recommendations (as the financial planner did in Chapter 5).

Remember that the consultants are there so that you can quickly gain their insights and then release them as soon as they have served that purpose. Research using the Internet, the library, and benchmarking may also be useful ways to capture appropriate knowledge for the strategic plan. The approach that most often takes the most time, is most costly with the highest risk of poor results is developing the results through internal research although it may be the way to get what is needed for the business.

The current status of the business is typically captured in narrative form. It would be most appropriate to include some business level performance data. Is the business growing, flat, or declining from several perspectives? Is the operation technically and method-wise cutting-edge or lagging our competition? Note the state of the workforce. Keep the description of the current situation to one page (12-point type) or less.

As difficult as it may be for the authors, it must be kept clear and concise. It must also be accurate, realistic and yet positive. Being the first team effort Core Team members will need to be patient and learn to work together in this mode. Be assured there will be several iterations of brainstorming, consolidating and then enhancing the current situation.

Keep smiling and sending those doing the documentation, (one or two members of the Core Team) back for more homework until they have captured the essence of the current situation with a sense of how the business got to its present state.

An effective method of operation for the Core Team is to brainstorm a topic with one member documenting the ideas. He then translates the notes outside of the meeting into a document that is to be a part of the strategic plan. He presents this draft at the next Core Team meeting for affirmation (what do you like about it) and enhancement (how could it be improved).

At the next meeting he presents draft two and so on until the Core Team accepts it in the latest draft form. I refer to this cycle as the Do/Present/Enhance cycle. Normally during a two-hour session, the current situation can be addressed and assigned for documentation in less than an hour. Then the Core Team can address the next item, which would be the mission statement.

Typically, at least two or three major items can be addressed in a two-hour session. And it normally takes three to five iterations of each item before it can be put to rest as a draft for presentation at a rollout.

THE ENGINEERING DIVISION
Case of the Absent Director

In another example, a colleague in a major corporation where I was employed, approached me about taking his engineering division through the steps of the Strategic Way Process™ . Dwight had been spending most of his time in the past two years working on a corporate litigation. During that same time our company management had decided to consolidate much of the manufacturing process engineering staff into Dwight's division. The division was approaching four hundred engineers, technicians and support people. With his absentee leadership the division operation was in a great deal of turmoil. Nothing to do with his leadership, everything to do with his absence.

The operation was complex to manage having many engineering disciplines present serving multiple manufacturing organizations within the corporation. Dysfunction was clearly created when a number of engineering units from across the company were consolidated into Dwight's division. Each unit that came in brought with them their own leadership, their own unique work processes and their vision of how an engineering division should function. Not that anything was unacceptable about any of their leaders or their work processes or their vision for how the operation should function. It appeared to me like seeing oil mixed with water. Each unit was capable in their own way but not effective when thrown together.

In the first meeting with the selected leaders from across this mix of units, we began putting together a strategic plan, step one of the Strategic Way Process™ . Two leaders in the first meeting had their chairs turned sideways to avoid looking at me. That symbolized the frustration felt by most of these leaders. Most did not want to be in the conference room with this group. The tension in the room was obvious. I doubt that anyone expected a good outcome from this meeting.

Asking questions about the mission of the division, the vision of the ideal operation and so on through the first step, the group began to listen to one another. As we plowed through the strategic plan, they not only learned about one another, they gained each other's respect and a willingness to work together. They began to create an effective plan.

It was an interesting transformation from a group of leaders who were frustrated, lacked trust in one another and were feeling isolated to leaning in and beginning to really work together. The division strategic plan was rolled out t the division's workforce. The engineers, technicians and support staff were so pleased with and relieved in seeing this newly formed strategic plan. They were equally intrigued by the apparent unity of the unit directors. These engineers and techs were now expressing a significant degree of confidence that the ideal vision mapped out by the newly formed leadership was something of which they wanted to be a part.

When the last of the 6 steps of the Strategic Way Process were completed the leadership that was formed and the four hundred plus engineers and technicians were not only functioning well within this Strategically Optimized Management System but there was an amazing unity demonstrated. This level of unity is typically seen when the 6-step process is applied. Going through the Strategic Way Process turned what had been a highly dysfunctional operation into a well-managed high performing operation. Adding resources in this case did not improve the operation. In fact, it exacerbated the problem. Effective management of the existing operation is the answer to achieving the vision leaders have for their businesses.

Lesson Learn: *Where there is disunity, distrust of colleagues and process confusion, the Strategic Way Process resolves these issues extremely well.*

CRAFTING THE MISSION
Where we are going

The mission statement scopes the work of the business, to whom the work is directed, conditions of how the work will be done, and the benefit within and beyond the business of doing this work.

The mission and the yet to be determined ideal vision of carrying out the mission define the long-term destination of the business. The mission and vision are written with the intent that they will stand for decades.

The mission describes the primary work of the business. This is not the administration or other support work that must go on in every business, but the primary transformations that occur in taking the needs of those served and transforming those needs into the products and services which meet their needs.

Suppose a business buys vegetables from farmers, prepares them for retail consumption and distributes them to retail businesses. The mission statement might be *"We buy and process the freshest, certified as organic and locally grown vegetables for your retail market so that healthy choices are available to the consumer"*.

This statement gets to the heart of what this business is all about. The work is to buy and process, not grow, vegetables and not fruits or grains. Focusing on vegetables may allow the operation resources to be more focused, more competitive. It is further narrowed to vegetables certified to be organically grown and locally produced. None will be brought in from distant sources. The greater good, beyond the profit, is providing the consumer with healthy choices.

There are some considerations these business leaders need to address. Are the vegetables directed to retail outlets only, or could wholesalers or other entities become recipients? Will this market be there over the next several decades? Does limiting the market as noted allow the business to sufficiently focus its resources on meeting its long-term objectives. Yet it must not place limits that keep the business from expanding into logical future markets.

Finally, why is this work being done from a perspective beyond the obvious benefit to the workforce, investors, farmers and retailers? What is the benefit to the larger whole? This too may be included in the mission statement as it was in this example.

Steve Jobs wanted everyone to be able to benefit from the use of computers interfacing with ordinary people in a friendly, enjoyable way. George Eastman wanted everyone to be able to take pictures of family and friends without having to hire a professional photographer. Henry Ford wanted everyone to be able to have an automobile for personal transportation. This benefit to the larger whole may or may not be a part of your vision for your business. You be the judge.

Is it easy to define a mission statement? No! Is it important and very rewarding? Yes! Does it take five or six or seven iterations through the Do/Present /Enhance Work cycle? Most often! This will mark one of the growth periods for the Core Team. Some will be frustrated with the work-cycle concept or the difficulty of getting this into a few words or putting just the right constraint on the work or understanding why we even need a mission statement, or all of the above. By the way, the mission statement needs to be inspiring to the workforce and to the market. Stay steady with the process. Don't flinch.

The mission statement becomes a major guidepost as the business travels into the future. Coupled with the vision statement, this becomes the summary destination of the business. Much is yet to be done to put the necessary detail behind these two statements. These statements are essential for properly focusing the business. It is challenging, frustrating at times, but most rewarding. Learn to have a good time doing this work. No one else in the business can do this work. Might as well enjoy it.

WE WILL HAVE SUCCEEDED IF...
The ideal outcome of carrying out the mission

This is simply stating in list form the bottom-line results of carrying out the mission. This describes the ideal results. In contrast, the vision statement will describe the ideal operation that produces the results, that is, what the business ideally looks like carrying out the work. Both are futuristic and idealistic. Both are creating in the minds of the stakeholders an image of the destination the business is pursuing. This provides for the whole workforce the goal line to be pursued. It gets everyone on the same page.

Stakeholders refers to everyone who has a stake in the future of the business.

The mission statement determines the scope of the work of the business. This description of the results amplifies or clarifies the work by stating what you would see if the work referenced in the mission statement was ideally completed as intended. This list should appear under the mission statement when documented because it is so closely coupled to the mission.

The list is an expansion of the work noted in the mission, not specific but more in terms of usefulness to the market. A statement of the mission and its associated outcomes must generally be enough to hold for 10, 20 or more years, therefore the outcomes must be described from the view of the intent of the work stated in the mission.

If family financial planning is the work, then we will have succeeded if families are wisely managing their expenses, generating income that more than meets their expenses, are building wealth that is invested to provide a high level of security, etc. Henry Ford spoke of a car in every garage. George Eastman spoke of everyone being able to take pictures. Steve Jobs spoke of computers being designed such that everyone could use them. This is the tone of the list of outcomes.

Generating the list greatly expands the understanding of the mission. It also provides the opportunity to narrow the scope of the work stated in the mission. Here is where the business looks to decide whether to develop capability to deliver certain outcomes or if doing so would be diluting the focus of the business. As with the mission statement, this list provokes the leaders to consider whether to plan for certain outcomes or not. The list aids in clarifying the boundaries of the work of the business.

Setting boundaries is extremely important to a business. Down the road when there is great temptation to diversify into work that does not really fit with the core competencies, this list will prompt cause to think it through.

The list reflects a high standard for the outcomes the business is to deliver; it describes the ideal. In that sense it has the same flavor as the vision statement will have regarding the operation. The list casts a vision for the outcome the business is to generate and to what ideal standard.

CASTING THE VISION
Ideally how the operation looks in carrying out the mission

The mission statement clarifies the work of the business, to whom that work is directed and what is intended to be accomplished by doing so. The vision statement describes what the operation looks like while doing the work.

The vision is a description of the ideal future state. If we could look down on the operation of the business being carried out as described by the mission statement and successfully producing the desired outcomes, what would that operation look like ideally from the viewpoint of the stakeholders? That is the question that is answered with the vision statement.

Imagine a person deciding he can operate a better retail store than the one of which he just walked out. In his mind he sees a store where the prices are lower than other stores offering the same products. He visualizes enough checkout stations that lines are always short. He sees items for sale are well displayed. He sees a store that is spotlessly clean. He buys the store and is so successful as his vision is becoming a reality that he decides to open a second store and do the same with it. As the second store begins to achieve the same results as the first, he opens a third store.

Now he is thinking of one-stop shopping. He sees expanding the products and services the business provides. He invests in a computer system to optimize purchasing. After a time, he builds highly functional warehouses. Sound familiar? It started something like this with Sam Walton thinking futuristically about operating a better five-and ten-cent store. Go for your futuristic view of the business.

The mission, outcomes and vision combined become the target or destination the business will pursue for the long-term. The mission and vision guide the design, staffing and operation of the business.

Once committed to the mission and vision, the long-term objective of the business becomes carrying out the mission and achieving the vision–the Destination!

Why bother with vision? It clarifies what the business is to work toward. It brings unity to the thinking of the stakeholders. It sets a standard to work toward. It is up-lifting. It gives hope. It encourages. It focuses the resources. It adds significant value to being a part of the business. It makes decision making easier and of higher quality. Everyone wins!

The Core Team will need encouragement to think beyond the current situation. Visioning is typically not what they have been doing. It is not how the culture shapes thinking. Know this! The team will have to be encouraged to think future state, especially ideal future state. The team will want to get into the "how to," But that is for later in the strategic plan development. As Core Team members prompt one another to think beyond what is and into not only what could be but into what they want it to be, or ideally, need it to be.

Recipients of the products and services know what they want from the business. Ask those who work directly with them. The workers know what they need to get the work done and the leaders know what they want to achieve, the bottom line. Get in the shoes of each of those who have a stake in carrying out the mission and describe how they would like the operation to function and what the results should look like, ideally. It takes imagination and courage to describe it. It will take courage to commit to it. It will take great effort to achieve it. It will be worth it. Nothing less is acceptable.

The business leaders and ultimately the whole workforce will reference the mission time and time again, almost daily. It will be used as a guide in decision making. It will be used as a test to determine if everything is being addressed that should be addressed. It will be used to measure progress. It will be used to initiate change. It will be used as a reason for celebrations along the way.

The vision will light up the hearts and minds of the workers. It will demonstrate the positive outlook of the leaders. All of the stakeholders will share this vision and in unity work toward achieving it. The vision will be valued by all.

Carrying out the mission and achieving the vision clearly becomes the destination of the business.

And there is the rally cry to be considered. Not essential to be part of a strategic plan but may prove to be helpful in doing just that–Rallying the troops! You may wish to give it some attention in the Core Team or during the rollout of the strategic plan to the workforce. In a few words, what phrase would get everyone's attention regarding the mission and vision of the business.

When Xerox decided to put emphasis on working as a team within the business operation and with their customers they created the rally cry "Team Xerox". It had a twofold meaning reminding the workforce and their customers that they were team players. Very clever. It appeared as a huge banner stretched across their downtown Xerox high rise office building. And I am quite certain it was used within the workforce as well as with their customers. You may wish to seek a rally cry for your business.

SETTING THE VALUES
That which we must embrace to reach our destination

There are many values that exist within any given business. The values of interest here are those that must be embraced to carry out the mission and achieve the vision of the business. These values clearly are not currently as visible in the workforce culture as they need to be.

Every business has a set of esoteric values that must be embraced if the business is to carry out its mission and achieve its vision. If we are a construction company, do we need to value craftsmanship? I think so. If we are doctors do we need to value human life? Of course we do. If we are Christians do we need to value spiritual growth? It is a must. And so it goes with each unique business. These values need to be stated, defined and embraced.

There are also more general values that have great worth in most any business. Some that seem to be robust, that is, transcend the organization with great influence, such as demonstrating integrity in everything we do, treating everyone with respect, being good stewards of all resources we manage, doing everything with excellence, etc.

General values such as these need to be carefully selected. Ones that are not currently obvious in the work culture but needed if the business is to get to its destination. Values carefully selected, stated and embraced are essential to shaping the culture of a healthy, growing business. For a business to be truly functional, for there to be unity, there needs to be a common set of values. This removes dissension in the ranks and in the leadership. The synergistic effect of team can now transcend the organization.

The right values will promote a certain peace and joy no matter how difficult the task. People will be attracted to a business with a meaningful, positive set of values. Those that cannot embrace these values should not be hired or continue as part of the workforce.

Of the many values that could transcend an organization, identify those that need to be emphasized or introduced to create a culture that propels the organization toward its desired destination.

Here is an example of a set of values with a brief explanation.
- The one thing: Focus on the vision
- The real thing: Seek the truth
- The right thing: Choose right over expedient.

The rally cry: "One thing! Real thing! Right thing! I must admit this rally cry is a bit wordy. It may take time to come up with a rally cry. Don't let that hold up creation of the strategic plan.

There are also values that a business evolves that may well deter it from carrying out its mission and achieving its vision. Values such as loyalty and old friendships may be of this nature. Extreme embracement of these values may lead to keeping people in positions where they no longer or perhaps never did really added value to the business.

We all know about "The good old boys club." What do you think holds them together? Loyalty and old friendship may be at the heart of it. These can be and often are commendable values. But if miss-used, one or more may no longer be adding much collective value.

There may be people in the business that are working hard with knowledge and skill in their areas yet cannot earn their way into the positions held by the good old boys. This is like a rotting cancerous wound in the business. Sound harsh! Everyone knows about it. Because of someone's relationship with someone in control they are kept in place. You may not progress satisfactorily toward the mission and vision with this kind of diseased organization.

Neither are the good old boys in a healthy place. They need to be in jobs where they fit, where they can add value, where they can build capability that leads to worth that can be legitimately rewarded. It may be an awkward and painful transition to move them out of their current position but best for the business and the good old boys.

A value that should be given consideration is the value each person adds to the workforce as they seek to carry out the mission and achieve the vision. Give great importance to putting people in positions or roles where their knowledge and skills fit carrying out the functions of their position and they have strong interest and passion for this role. This is vital to establishing a healthy organization. The career-matching step in Chapter 6 addresses this issue.

The Core Team now turns in the strategic planning process to how to get from the Current Situation to the destination. What approaches will be developed to get there. These approaches are referred to as strategies.

DRAFTING THE BUSINESS LEVEL STRATEGIES
The approaches to reaching the destination

Strategies are a plan of action to reach the destination. The current situation is where we are now. Our destination is to carry out the business mission and achieve the vision. To get the business from the current situation to the destination there needs to be well thought out approaches to get there. These approaches are referred to as strategies.

Suppose the business distributes fresh, organic vegetables. The market is the Boston area. A strategy would be to contract with farms within 200 miles. The vegetables will be transported by refrigerated truck at night for sale that day. Only certified organic farms will be considered. Are there any more decisions to make? Of course, there are many. So where does all this end?

Strategy should begin with the broadest considerations to be addressed in the business level strategic plan. After addressing the business level strategy, there is an expansion of these strategies at the Key Result Area (KRA) level, the next lower level. This will be reviewed in Chapter 7.

More detailed strategies at this level would be contracting trucking companies that could provide the required transportation. Determining delivery schedules, etc. The strategies at business level need to be threshed out by the Core Team with counsel from the Resource Group if helpful and rolled out to the whole workforce if appropriate. Strategies may be proprietary limiting their review to only those that need to know.

Is the strategy chosen always the best path to the destination? Probably not, and that prompts the initiation of challenges to the strategy, sometimes during the year and always on an annual basis.

There are three basic reasons to prompt a need for changing one or more strategies:

1. Something has been learned from within or external to the business operation that suggests change
2. The situation or environment that the business works within has changed since the strategy was formed
3. Progress toward the destination is not satisfactory with the current strategies.

In my experience with a wide spectrum of businesses, the leaders should see their strategy change from ten to thirty percent annually. Mission, vision and values have long lives mainly because they are not situation dependent and are somewhat idealistic.

Because strategies evolve, the first step in developing them may be to document what strategies the business is currently using. Once this is organized on paper, the Core Team can see how to improve it. Exposure to the workforce, if appropriate, will yield affirmation of Core Team developed strategies and often include suggestions for further improvement. All of this analysis will likely lead to interest in what other businesses are doing including similar businesses not competing in the same region, direct competitors, universities, etc.

A weakness often seen in businesses is failing to seek available information external to the business operation when seeking to improve the strategies and the processes of the business. Think of the story of the financial planner in Chapter 5. As the consultant, I prompted Dwight to seek out a consultant outside of his market to assess his operation and make recommendations. It revolutionized his operation.

Strategic development is a great place for the Core Team to bring in people from the Resource Group. As they come in, ground them in the work done so far, the mission, outcomes, vision and values and then the strategy developed so far. Then challenge them to offer insights applicable to the strategy development. This invariably produces new and useful insights. Thank them for their thoughts indicating they may well be called upon in the future and that they will be acknowledged for their contribution.

Strategic planning can be the motivator needed for moving the business toward the mission and vision at a more acceptable rate. A healthy business is constantly seeking an orderly change in its strategy to make more and better progress down the path to their destination. Several iterations by the Core Team of the Do/Present/Enhance cycle are normal to reach a point where the team is ready to move on to measures.

DEFINING THE MEASURES OF PROGRESS
How we measure progress toward the destination

Suppose you were the manager responsible for the operation of a golf course but you had to sit in a room at the clubhouse with the door closed at all times. What is the minimal information you would want slipped under the door each month for you to be confident in knowing that satisfactory progress was being made toward the mission and vision of the course?

Bottom line, what is the net income of the course per month, sales revenue less expenses? Is there a high regard for playing the course by its participants? Is the pro shop a friendly well-run operation? What is the shape of the course and is it being cared for efficiently? Are we gaining market share? What is the attitude of the staff and the management? Etc.

Is the manager of any golf course or business satisfied with opinions or do they want facts? What if the opinions are different depending on who voices them? Who should one believe? Is it okay to have all this delivered in a sheaf of paper an inch thick? No trends, no repeating formats, lots of detail to sift through, no conclusions or summary data which would save hours trying to understand? Not at all acceptable!

Measures of progress should be summarized on one page.
Anything more is half done.

Mangers need concise, comprehensive. timely, consistently formatted progress data. So does the whole workforce. Remember that the whole business team needs to know the movement forward throughout the journey. Everyone is then motivated to keep doing what contributes most to making good progress and to pursue improvements in what each does.

Information that profiles the progress of the business toward the mission and vision is needed for everyone, not just the leadership, but the rest of the workforce as well.

Often managers and floor workers alike feel they have inadequate information concerning progress whether the operation is a golf course, manufacture of widgets, a nonprofit or a medical clinic. Many times, there is little understanding of how to measure and feedback performance information about the operation in a timely and useful manner. This is essential to move the business toward the destination at an acceptable pace.

The first step in developing a well-designed performance management system is to determine the 8 to 12 business level measures that describe the performance of the business. Typically half should describe the end or "bottom line" results of the operation. These measures lag the operation period such as month, quarter or year. The other half of the measures should describe key performance indicators during the operation of the business that will predict the bottom line results. The creative work lies in being comprehensive and in getting the leading and lagging measures to correlate. If the leading indicators are doing well, does this accurately predict lagging indicators? If yes, then we know what to focus on during the operation to get the desired end results.

Suppose there is a significant number of clients working with the attorneys in a law firm during any one month. This measure is intended to predict a high level of hours logged by the end of the month translating to a high level of fees accumulated. Is that the case at the end of the month? If yes, there is a correlation between number of clients and that month's revenue. If not, there is not a correlation with the lagging indicator, monthly revenue. Further development of leading indicators is needed.

There is a need to draw conclusions from relevant progress data effectively presented, not subjective opinion, a very significant shift for some businesses.

Once a set or system of measures is defined, the next step is to collect the data, process it so that it can be fed back in a timely, meaningful format to those that need to be encouraged and can effect change to improve the operation when appropriate. This step will be dealt with in more detail in Appendix B Step 6 task to develop a performance management system. For now, a list of the business level measures is sufficient. Expect this list to evolve and stabilize over time.

The idea of 8 to 12 measures to describe the performance of the operation will intrigue the Core Team. The team members may not get very far in actually determining this set. Don't dwell on it. The business level management team will be in a better position to do this when they get to Step 6 of the Strategic Way Process™. They will have gotten insight from the previous steps. But it is worth the effort to make a run at it at this time.

THE MANUFACTURING PLANT UNIT COST
Making a Buck

The effective use of measures cannot be overvalued. The following client story was my first venture into management consulting. It illustrates the value of establishing and applying comprehensive measures in a business.

A new plant manager stepped into my office initiating a dramatic improvement in the management of a manufacturing plant and an equally significant change in the direction of my career. Mike wasn't aware of this happening and neither was I.

At the time I was directing the completion of a significant portion of a plant where Mike had just been appointed as plant manager. The plant had been making product for sale for some time. Significant money was being spent in this final stage to implement all of the planned innovations. When completed this manufacturing plant would be state of the art.

This facility was the sole supplier of product to a 10-year-old business within a blue-chip corporation. The product was well received in the market place and sales volume was steadily increasing. While cutting edge technology was being applied to this manufacturing plant the business was losing money. The cost to produce a unit of the product was greater than the sale price.

Mike told me that corporate headquarters had sent a clear message. If the business didn't "Make a Buck" within a year, that is, make a profit, the business would be terminated and the plant closed even though the business was integral to the corporation's future plans.

Mike was seeking the counsel of his department heads managing the operation and the unit directors supplying technology for completion of the plant. He was asking a simple question.

What needs to be done to continue making good product, complete the final phase of the plant development and to "Make a Buck" within a year?

Out of curiosity, I had just attended a two-hour seminar describing a way of improving how one manages a business operation. The seminar speaker was part of the management team of a major division of a blue-chip company in the south. His management team was noted for their innovativeness and success in managing their operation.

Using what I had just heard at the two-hour seminar, I briefly suggested a process based upon my translation of concepts I recalled from the seminar. Mike thanked me and left.

A week later Mike knocked at my door again. He said he had spoken with his department heads and all of the technology unit directors. He surmised that I had the answer to how to make a buck within a year. He asked if I would come work for him to implement the suggested process.

I was intrigued by the concepts I had just learned from the seminar and was challenged to put them into use in a real live application. I told Mike I would facilitate the process I had proposed. I noted that I could still continue with my role as unit director. He agreed.

In nine months, I had guided the implementation of the concepts I had learned at the seminar. The plant was now very near completion, production volume was steadily increasing and meeting sales demand. The business was "Making a Buck" well within the one year deadline! The business was now profitable and went on to be a most successful enterprise within the corporation.

When Mike first approached me not only was the business losing money but an inexperienced manager had been appointed to direct one of the key departments, final assembly. I saw Karen years later when we happened to be on the same plane while both on business trips. She confessed that she had no idea of how to responsibly bring down costs in this department that was new to her. Karen said she would have lost her job if I had not brought in that process. It was most rewarding to me to be a part of saving a valued business. I was also pleased that I was able to assist someone new to that level of management.

I knew very little about the management of this manufacturing plant. Yes, I understood technically how the automated processes functioned because of my involvement in delivering the technology, but not the contributions to unit cost or many other aspects of the management functions. The role I played was to facilitate a portion of the process I now use as a part of the Strategic Way Process™. The concepts used to effectively reduce costs at this manufacturing plant in a responsible way has broad application in any kind of business.

Reflecting on this situation, the planned innovations were not yet completed. The new plant manager was not familiar with the manufacturing process. The assembly department, a major contributor to unit cost, had a new manager. Due to manufacturing costs the business was losing money and I was offering a process of which I had just been exposed. Sound impossible to work through this situation and meet the goal of making a buck within a year? Well, we did!

At the seminar the presenter had suggested that developing progress measures was a key element in strategic planning. These measures needed to be comprehensive and relevant in describing the state of the operation. The presenter claimed that these measures would allow effective management of the operation.

With this insight I envisioned that if I were responsible for an operation and was locked in a conference room I would need to know specific information about its progress slipped under the door, let's say, once a month. Presenting this scenario gave the plant manager and his department heads a means to test the effectiveness of the measures.

To make the measures useful and timely I would want eight to twelve measure that were comprehensive. Mike agreed to my approach. I then told Mike to huddle with his department heads and define those measures. They came up with twelve measures. Mike took them to the business manager. He agreed with their set of measures saying that, in fact, he would like them reported to him on a regular basis from this point on.

I then asked the department heads to follow the same scenario, that is, if they were locked in a room, what eight to twelve performance measures slipped under the door monthly would give them an accurate picture of their department's performance. They came back with measures that were the same as the plant measures where applicable, such as contribution to unit cost, product produced, etc. But some were peculiar to their department as one would expect. After some discussion the plant manager and department heads agreed on all of these department level measures.

At this point I asked the department heads to determine the current value of each of their department measures. Then the plant manager used the collective department data and some unique plant level data to determine the current value of the plant measures. This became the baseline performance of the departments and the plant as a whole.

From this baseline data, I asked Mike to set goals for the plant level measures that would bring the unit cost down to the level where the business was "Making a Buck." After Mike gave this much thought and consultation with the department heads, he determined the plant goals. I then directed the department heads to set goals at department level that would meet the plant goals. The discussions thus far were fostering very meaningful interaction between the new plant manager and the department heads, an added positive benefit of this process.

I next directed the department heads to go to their own people and to the technology units completing the plant and find out how they could contribute to closing the gap between the goals and the baselines and at what cost. Bingo! Everyone was now focused on how to "Make a Buck", produce the needed quantity and quality of product and complete the development of the plant.

The department heads determined the most effective gap closures in consultation with their people and with the technology unit directors. These gap closure plans were then agreed upon by the plant manager and fellow department heads collectively. From there the department heads and the technology unit directors were charged with carrying out the gap closure work and only that work. Spend no money beyond those limits.

In nine months, the plant unit costs were reduced to the point where the business was "Making a Buck", quality product was being shipped to customers in sufficient volume to meet the growing demand, the plant was rapidly being completed and everyone was participating in the solution. All done with progress measure. The plant manager and the department heads continued to use these measures in the ongoing management of the plant.

Never underestimate the power of progress measures.

INSIGHTS ILLUSTRATED
What we can learn from these client stories

Effective communication of the strategic plan from top leaders down to people on the work floor is key to successful implementation of a strategic plan. Leaders should look for every opportunity to reference the plan in their discussions and to communicate the plan at every opportunity. From presentations by leaders to one-on-one conversations, the strategic plan should routinely enter into discussions about the work at hand.

Questions that may be asked: Is this activity consistent with the plan? Are we within the scope of the mission? Is this resolution of an issue within the plan's strategies? Will this strategy get us to the vision? With new insights, is there cause to modify the plan strategy? Are we making satisfactory progress toward the vision?

Don't accept the organization's current situation. Leverage your strengths as never before. Identify and turn your weaknesses into strengths. Seize the opportunities that cross your path. Turn threats into advantages.

The Leaders program is an illustration of an abundance of knowledge and skill pooled together but lacking an understanding of how to organize in a way that moves implementation forward. A lack of unity in the leadership found highly capable people pulling in different directions. Outcomes of carrying out the mission were not identified and clearly defined as key result areas.

Senior professors at one of the top universities in the country working with top managers from eleven blue chip companies represented a rare combination of talent. There was a strong commitment to this program by these gifted people combined with strong backing from their organizations, yet they were stuck on how to take the next step from mission/vision to implementation. The

Strategic Way Process guided them to a successful implementation of this unique and complex program.

Again, much credit must be given to the program coordinators, MIT senior professors Kent Bowen and Tom Magnanti, for the vision they cast of such an important program and for being humble enough to seek help in bringing them through the program's roadblocks.

THE STRATEGIC WAY PROCESS ROLLOUT OF THE STRATEGIC PLAN
Engage the whole workforce

When a team has completed work that needs to be understood, enhanced, owned, accepted by and complied with by a group of people, an effective process to accomplish this is a Strategic Way Process Rollout which will be referred to simply as a Rollout.

A Rollout involves a brief presentation of the results of the team's work, the "Rollout". This presentation would be to an audience affected by this work followed by solicitation from the audience of what is liked about the work and suggestions for how the work can be enhanced. Case in point is a team's newly drafted business level strategic plan.

The Core Team will have put a great deal of effort into developing a strategic plan. The plan will describe the businesses' current situation, a well-crafted mission statement, a word picture drawn of a vision of the ideal operation with outcomes identified and a set of values the workforce needs to embrace, a developed set of strategies and a clearly defined set of progress measures.

The audience will most likely never have seen such a well thought out long range plan. In my years of experience doing rollouts, the audience will be delighted, encouraged and inspired. Likewise the Core Team will now be reflecting upon the valuable step that has been taken in the management of the business. The Core Team will be greatly encouraged by the positive response of the audience.

For the Rollout the Core Team needs to put their work in concise clear form to be presented in about twenty minutes. Keep the presentation simple in concept, not a lot of detail although more detail will have been generated earlier by the Core Team to provide adequate insight for successful implementation.

The audience needs to first understand the big picture, an overview in 20 minutes. They will learn more of the detail during implementation of the strategic plan. Mark the presentation material as Draft. It needs to be easy to assimilate and appear open to enhancement. If the audience senses they may be given the opportunity to influence the plan they will feel ownership in it, very important to implementation. Have two members of the Core Team present the material with the rest of the team up front to demonstrate unity and commitment. Projecting the presentation onto a screen or displaying it on a wall keeps the audience all focused on the slides as they are presented.

For the sake of simplicity let us assume the business work force consists of one hundred and fifty or less people. For larger organizations follow the concepts described here but do several Rollouts. For example, a rollout by division or department.

The best environment I have experienced for getting a positive response "Roll-In" from the audience is found in dividing the workforce into small groups after the presentation. In these small groups each person is given a safe place away from the other groups with sufficient air time to express their views about the presentation team's work, in this case the Core Team.

Three members of each small group are given assignments. One is to facilitate the small group agenda, another to act as scribe, that is, to cryptically document the group's comments and a third to use the scribed notes to report back their comments later when the small groups are reassembled into one large group.

The facilitator's role is to walk down through the presentation material that is in hard copy in front of each member of the small group asking two questions: 1. What do you like about it? How could it be enhanced? The scribe is making cryptic notes of the responses. The reporter will use these notes when presenting back to the reassembled audience.

With the Rollout of the business strategic plan each group facilitator would ask their group: What do you like about the Current Situation? When the group becomes quiet again ask: How would you enhance it? Be sure the scribe is taking notes. Cryptic notes!

The facilitator should always respond positively to an enhancement with a "thank you." One in the small group may say "white" and another may say "black". Smile and say thank you to both. The decision of whether to incorporate either will be made by the presenting team at a later date. Now is the time to foster participation not judgement.

The small group facilitator must immediately stop any one in the small group from being critical of the presented work. This is garbage dumping and is not constructive. An effective approach is for the facilitator to put her hand up with palm facing the critic and saying, "Now is not the time to be critical. If you have an enhancement to the presented material that would be most welcome."

The facilitator then moves on to the mission statement presented using the same two questions. This followed by the outcomes list and so on through the whole presentation of the strategic plan.

During this small group time the presenting team circulates among the groups answering any questions they may have in understanding the presentation material and assuring that the group member's three designated roles are being carried out.

When the small groups have contributed all of their affirmations and enhancements, reassemble the small groups into one large group again. The reporter from each small group will highlight one by one the likes and enhancements of their group to the reassembled audience using their scribe's notes.

Give the reporters no more than three or four minutes to present to assure that it is highlights they are presenting and to allow time for every group to be heard. On a light note threaten to hook them off the stage if they get to voluminous.

Now the audience is hearing more about what is good about the Core Team's work and witnessing a clear demonstration of the willingness of the Core Team to consider suggested enhancements.

Two important responsibility have been given to the audience through these small groups: Acknowledge what is liked about the work, find where the work is lacking and offer solutions in the form of enhancements. No negative garbage dumping has been allowed, that is, just criticism of the work. When negativism occurs, the facilitators note that only likes or enhancements are being sought. Facilitators need to be firm about it.

Rollouts always reveal what resonates with the audience. This gives the presenting team encouragement and confidence in the work they have done. It also makes a giant step in bringing unity within the audience regarding this work.

Ownership comes from understanding and from being given the opportunity to offer enhancements to the work. Never underestimate the power of Rollouts.

And there are always some great ideas captured from the suggested enhancements. No matter how long the presenting team has worked on a task the rollout typically produces some great enhancements.

With the opportunity to note what is liked and how it can be enhanced the audience is well on its way to acceptance of the team's work. Even the most ardent naysayer will have to concede that the work of the team is worthy of consideration and some level of acceptance. In the Rollout process the audience has gained a new dimension in the role of being a business team member.

To legitimize a rollout, the team must promise to go back and consider every point in the feedback provided by the small groups. The audience must be assured that some though not necessarily all of the suggested enhancements will be incorporated in the final draft of the team's work. At some future date in some recognized way the team must confirm that this has happened. This will be the wrap-up of the rollout.

A Rollout needs to be done in a series. A rollout to present the business level strategic plan may first be held with all of the business level leaders, then the Resource Group, and then after consideration of the enhancements, to the leaders at the next level down in the organization and so on to the floor-level workforce. This is a great opportunity to honor the leadership at the various levels as well as the floor-level people.

The next opportunity to do a rollout is after the series of roll-outs is complete for the strategic plan. This occurs when steps two and three of the Strategic Way Process are complete. This work will be of as much interest to the whole workforce as was the strategic plan. They will have experienced a Rollout and should be made aware that the organization optimization and matching process has been done. Those subjects will perk their interest! And it will demonstrate a clear commitment by the leadership to implement the strategic plan.

THE BUSINESS STRATEGIC PLAN
AND ITS USES
Why create long range plans

The business strategic plan describes the destination of the business through the mission and vision statements, the path to get there through the values and strategy, and how to measure the progress along the way. The description is concise, clear and complete. Leaders need to continuously refer to this destination and path to get there in everything that is done in the business from this point on.

The strategic plan focuses the resources toward the work and the object of that work defined in the mission, to the approach described by the strategy, embracing the values that will reshape the culture so that the business may enjoy uncapped, healthy growth capability.

Uncapped healthy growth capability is a highly desirable business outcome.

From business strategic plan to the processes on the work floor think in terms of growing to at least three to five times current capacity. Too often I see businesses planning toward only twenty or thirty percent growth with the current processes needing redesign when the planned capacity has been reached. Think big! It will pay off in reduced time by not having to do additional process redesign.

When products and services are added, deleted or modified, the business level strategic plan guides the process. When the operation that produces the products and services is modified, the plan guides this work. When staff are recruited, trained or released, the plan provides guidance. In operation of all the processes of the business, the plan acts as a guide. Everything is to be done within the framework of the strategic plan.

The business level strategic plan is kept in front of all stakeholders, namely, the employees, suppliers and investors of the business. Let it be known that this is where we are going, this is how we will get there, and this is how we measure progress along the way. It is a powerful, uplifting message that focuses all resources.

This is real leadership. Without this plan, with good intentions, the stakeholders will tend to head in slightly or significantly different directions. The strategic plan allows decisions to be made every day by the stakeholders within a framework that brings synergy to the use of all resources. This accelerates the operation in moving toward the destination.

The business level strategic plan provides the necessary umbrella to optimize the organization structure, match careers to positions, develop the Key Result Area strategic plans, the team building and the progress performance system. All of these efforts that follow are guided by the business strategic plan.

There are three areas of the business level strategic plan that will evolve with time. The current situation changes when the workforce gains new insights about the operation and as the environment changes while the business is moving forward. The strategy may then need to be modified in response to these changes. And the corporate measures may change as the leaders learn to better define the leading and lagging indicators and their correlation.

These evolving changes are typically addressed annually half way through the calendar year. The annual plan is typically prepared just prior to the beginning of the calendar year. This separates the annual and strategic planning efforts by 6 months.

Everyone will appreciate the spreading of the planning workload. However, this does not preclude changes to the strategic plan at any time during the year when it is deemed appropriate.

When the business strategic plan is readied by the Core Team, it is time to roll out this piece of work by the Core Team to the leadership of the business, the Resource Group and then to the whole workforce. When the enhancements have been either incorporated, or discarded, the strategic plan should now be available for the leaders and the work floor workers for guidance in their daily work. As described previously, a war room is one of several ways to do so.

Completing the strategic plan at business level is a major step. It has been well thought out by the Core Team, is complete in its content. It incorporates insights from the business leaders not part of the Core team and from the Resource Group. It also factors in research that may have been carried out within or outside of the business. It has been understood and enhanced by the floor workers. Overall it is of great interest to the whole workforce and has become owned by them.

Leadership is taking people where they would otherwise not go. Strategic planning is a manifestation of leadership.

The development of the strategic plan completes step one of the Strategic Way Process™. Much has been accomplished by the business leaders. A clear direction has been set. It is time to clear the way for the plan to be implemented. The next 5 chapters do just that. All necessary for the business leaders and the whole workforce to effectively implement the strategic plan.

STEP 2-OPTIMALLY STRUCTURED

Streamline the Workflow

The Strategic Way Process Steps:
    Strategically Driven
    Optimally Structured–You are here
    Career Matched
    Strategically Implemented
    Team Operated
    Progress Managed

The objective of this chapter is to optimize the organization structure for the implementation of the newly developed strategic plan. The existing structure is often less than optimal. The structure has most likely evolved over time as the business changes due to innovation in the operation, changing technology, changes to the products and services, changes in leadership as well as other issues.

The view of what is an appropriate organization structure is likely embedded in the business culture. A fresh look at the structure may result in small changes or perhaps some more significant.

All structure changes are to improve the ability of the operation to accelerate progress toward the destination–the mission and vision.

The Core Team should read this chapter just prior to having the facilitator walk the team through this step. The Appendix B Task to carry out step 2 defines for the facilitator the process guidelines for optimizing the organization structure. The narrative that follows here will describe concepts and insights to be considered by the leaders while carrying out this step.

CLARIFY THE WORK OF THE OPERATION
Transformations vs. Transactions

When addressing the issues of structure optimization, one should consider transformations versus transactions. This may add greater understanding of the work of the business and ultimately allow the work to be structurally organized more effectively.

In any business client needs are transformed into delivered products and services or outcomes of carrying out the mission of the business. These are the primary functions of the business. There are many transformations that occur within these major transformation.

In a business that makes widgets of some kind, client needs may be transformed through sales into sales orders. The sales orders would then be transformed into factory work orders. The work orders transformed into resources procured to produce the widgets that meet the client needs. The widgets are then delivered to the client. All are transformations. The terms may be different for different types of businesses but the concepts are the same whether making widgets or delivering professional services or anything in between.

In contrast, transactions are auxiliary functions to support carrying out the transformations. Examples include accounting, legal counsel, human resource functions, inventory movement, research and development, even leadership and management functions. All should be focused on fostering the effectiveness of the groups that are making the transformations.

Those who carry out the transactions are serving those who carry out the transformations. If we could make the transformations without accountants, attorneys, HR, inventory movement,

R&D, leaders and managers, we would. Ouch! None of them transform client needs into products and services.

Transformation is what a business is all about.

So, do we eliminate these people doing transactional work? No, we need them, we respect and value them, but we want them to think of themselves as servants. They are serving the processes making the transformations.

Think of those carrying out the transformations as outsourcing within the business some services the transaction groups need in order to function more effectively. To the service groups, the transformation groups are their clients. The transformation groups should be treated as clients by the transactional groups. *We are here to serve you.* I have seen this reversed in too many business operations. Some of you in transformational work know exactly of which I speak.

This approach to understanding the work may well change the view of the Core Team and the rest of the workforce when exposed to these concepts. These concepts are not meant to be a threat to anyone or diminish anyone's role, but rather to provide a healthier perspective on how each work group serves to make progress toward the destination–the mission and vision of the business.

When discussing these concepts, I suggest you develop a work flow chart to help everyone better see the role they play–where they fit in. This would show workflow graphically displaying the stages of transformation of the client needs into delivered products and services. Putting the service groups under the flow of the transformation groups graphically represents their supporting role to the transformation groups. There is nothing like a graphic to convey these relationships.

With the Core Team discussion of transformations and transactions, the development of a work flow graphic will easily evolve. More often than not I have experienced the whole workforce responding very positively to this graphic which they are typically seeing for the first time. I encourage taking the time to create such a graphic. The flow chart will also guide the Core Team in the grouping of functions into areas, a central concept applied in the organization optimization process.

KEY RESULT AREAS
Synergistic grouping of business functions

With agreement on the natural flow of the work, the next step is to group the functions. I have seen a major manufacturer put all those doing transformational work for a product line in one building. From sales to shipping housed together. The communications were outstanding. Everyone recognized the important value of carrying out their function. It worked for them. May work for some but not for other businesses.

Another major manufacturer will put a common transformation to many product lines in one area or building. This transformation then serves many product lines. In large corporations this is often done. And with this approach there is the opportunity for effectiveness in carrying out that function. And with it the potential for getting disconnected from each of the product lines it serves. What is best for any particular business is in the hands of the business leaders for that business.

Today with the availability of the internet there is the opportunity for workers to perform transformational functions out of individual offices set up in their homes. This removes the business expense of brick and mortar buildings. This can also be advantageous for the workers by reducing personal expenses in the form of transportation costs and time traveling to an office building. This is likely to be very attractive to the employees. It may make it practical to take care of children while being "at work". I am familiar with a general insurance agency where all of the employees including the owner operate out of their homes. As the business grows all that is required of the owner is to set up an office in one room of the home of someone added to the workforce.

Essential to this form of operation is an excellent computer and telephone system tying the workforce together.

Most often I see functions formally grouped to address a number of issues in delivering products and services. The groups may be in different building, cities or even countries. In small to medium sized businesses the whole operation may be in one building or even on one floor. Here is where the uniqueness of the business comes into play.

When the functions at business level are placed in three to eight logically formed groups, depending on the complexity of the operation, each grouping may be recognized as a Key Result Area (KRA). The expectation is that it is key that each of these groups of functions be carried out well with steadily increasing positive results for the business to reach its destination–its mission and vision.

KRAs and the functions they include are at the heart of the design of the organization structure. There are many things to consider when grouping the functions that form these areas.

Functions that are highly dependent on one another need to be considered, that is, is there significant interconnectedness as they are carried out. A KRA may then best deal with the interrelated issues that arise in carrying out these functions. An example may be sales and marketing; marketing feeds sales and sales feeds marketing. The movement of physical parts and products often require that they be placed within close proximity. Parts manufacture are often placed close to the assembly operation.

Transactional functions that are common to most of the areas may be done best by putting them into a single KRA. Examples in the work flow could be engineering, human resources, research and development, accounting, legal, etc.

Although common to most areas, it may not always be good design to separate them into another area. An example is quality assurance. It may be best that each area team be responsible for the quality of carrying out the functions they provide within the workflow.

Physical location of the KRA's with respect to one another should be considered to allow team-to-team interaction. Research and Development may need to be physically near the area team to which it provides the most support. In a multi-national corporation, the areas may be North America vs Europe vs Asia, etc. In a small business the areas may be office vs manufacturing plant vs laboratory, etc. The area considerations apply to any size of organization.

Well-formed and functioning area teams determine how well the business moves along the path toward its destination—its mission and vision. This fine-tuning of the area structure and operation is an ongoing task.

This is also an appropriate time to think about any functions that would best serve the business by being out-sourced. Questions should arise about whether to use a service group doing transactional work be in-house or to outsource. Do payroll in-house or let a firm specializing in payroll do it? Same for Human Resource, legal, etc. Thoughtfully make these decisions. Who can best carry out the functions, short and long term?

Consider out-sourcing both the production of some part of the products and services and any other appropriate function within the operation. A business should become excellent at choosing what to do in-house and excellent at doing those functions. And being wise in knowing what and how to outsource, what to avoid doing directly and excellent at choosing between the options.

And what about leadership and management functions? Do we need people who spend most of their time carrying out leadership and management functions? If the business had the correct direction and the operation was aligned with it, there would be no need for business leadership positions. Because the direction of the business needs to be driven strategically and the client needs or competitive environment changes and new insights are learned about how to operate, it requires business leadership to be in place.

For the most part, people in the transformational functions are focused on just that, making the transformations. The management functions include long term and day-to-day operation of the business, so management is most likely here to stay. Therefore, it is likely that a business will need some people who spend most of their time, if not all, carrying out leadership and management functions.

It is appropriate when optimizing the organization structure to consider the core competencies that must be in place for the business to get to its destination, the mission and vision. What capability must be developed in-house, around which the current and future products and services will be produced and delivered? Look for these competencies in the primary workflow. These competencies are critical assets of the business and must be carefully nurtured.

THE MIT LEADERS FOR
MANUFACTURING PROGRAM
A 5-year program stalled after 6 months of development

An inspiring vision had been cast at a top-level university for bringing manufacturing back to the United States. This story describes the development of a management system to be operated by a diverse group of leaders representing both the university and 11 blue chip companies funding the program. As you will observe, an awesome vision is not enough.

At the Massachusetts Institute of Technology (MIT), the management and engineering schools in cooperation with 11 blue-chip companies launched a significant five-year program. The vision for this program was to take the best and brightest students with undergraduate science and engineering degrees and place them in a yet to be developed 24-month dual Master degree program. One Master degree in each student's technical field and the other in management.

MIT agreed to modify its curriculum to develop this dual master program. The eleven blue chip companies would fund the program and then seek to hire the program's graduates. With mentoring at high levels within the companies, these graduates would earn their way into highly influential company leadership positions. A long-term goal would be for this talent to help return world leadership in manufacturing to the United States. This program was intended to become a prototype for other universities and companies across the country. The program was to be called Leaders for Manufacturing.

The executives from the 11 companies had collectively agreed to fund the 5-year program with 46 million dollars. That's not exactly small change. The top management of the 11 companies believed these graduates would have a significant influence on their ability to gain back manufacturing market share.

MIT leadership believed they could supply the leaders and educate them to fulfill the participating company's expectations. MIT would recruit the best and brightest students to participate in this dual Master degree program. This program would require 5 highly regarded senior professors to dedicate significant time on this program to develop innovative curriculum to prepare the best and brightest students for carrying out the needed leadership roles in the 11 companies. These students would have engineering and science under-graduate degrees.

The eleven companies would seek out the graduates and provide avenues for them to navigate into positions of significant influence within each of their organizations. The top management would assure that these graduates got the appropriate guidance as they earned their way up through the management ranks of their corporate organizations.

A governing board was formed made up of an executive from each of the eleven companies and the equivalent leadership from MIT. This board was established to ensure the program's vision was achieved. Five senior professors from MIT and a high-level manager from each of the companies were organized into an operations team to develop over five years whatever was necessary within each company and at MIT to make this program successful. The operations team was meeting at the university two days per month to implement the program, a heavy investment of the team member's time.

The executives and managers were in complete unity concerning the vision for the program. After 6 months of program development, however, there was no movement forward. They had an inspiring vision and mission statement but were not able to form and execute the next step toward implementation. I was brought in to see if I could help the operations team move the program forward. At once I saw a combination of 16 top managers and educators of exceptional capability who had made a strong commitment to the common vision but nevertheless could not agree on how to take the next step to implement the program.

The members of the operating team were strongly motivated high achievers in their careers viewing their time as valuable. Collectively the team had the authority to call upon the resources of one of the top educational institutions in the country and the necessary resources from eleven leading manufacturing firms. Yet without a clearly and completely defined strategic plan for the program and its implementation they were unable to move forward.

I was employed at one of the eleven companies participating in this program. Rowley, the executive vice president of my company telephoned me describing the program of which he was a member of the governing board and the stalled situation the operations team were experiencing. Rowley asked me if I could help get the program moving again. I agreed to attend the next monthly meeting of the operations team.

On the first day of the two-day meeting I was introduced to the program co-directors, senior Professors Kent Bowen and Tom Magnanti (their actual names) and then to the operations team. After observing the state of the program over the two-day monthly session, I suggested to the co-directors that I could help them. They readily agreed to my offer to help.

When I got back to my home office, I explained to Vice President Rowley that I could help them implement the program. I wanted to know what amount of time I should commit to this program. He emphatically stated that he had committed far more funding for this program than any other single educational effort in the company's history. He was also convinced that this program would benefit our company more than any other investment of this type. He truly believed the Leaders Program would have a significant impact on our company's ability to be a leader in manufacturing. He clearly stated that I spend whatever amount of time needed to move the program forward. I got the picture!

On arrival at MIT the following month the co-directors indicated the operations team had agreed to give me the second full day with them. The first day was to address program administrative issues.

We began the second day's meeting at seven thirty in the morning with breaks at my discretion, ending the day at five in the afternoon. Lunch was brought in. These were clearly high achievers. They were eager to get through this impasse they had come up against. I began the meeting assuring them that I was solidly behind the mission and vision they had set out to achieve. I further noted that the mission and vision were an essential part of a strategic plan but that there was much more of the plan to be develop.

I explained to them that we needed to complete strategic planning. We needed to identify the key outcomes of carrying out the mission and achieving the vision. In this conference room, there were five senior professors, eleven high level managers representing their respective companies as well as four MIT staff members. Twenty people does not make for an easy to manage work group.

From the previous month's meeting, I had observed that most team members had some insight into strategic planning but apparently were not able to collectively apply these insights to this program. I also observed that there were two camps. One relating to planning within a manufacturing corporation and a second to planning in higher education. Neither camp could agree on what to develop next although there was complete agreement on the mission and vision. The program co-directors as well as the team were clearly frustrated.

I did a very simple thing to loosen up this somewhat polarized group. I had them count off around the table by twos. I sent the "one's" to one room and the "twos to another. This simple action arbitrarily mixed the two polarized groups into two working groups. Each group's task was to identify the key outcomes or functional areas that needed to be developed within MIT and the companies in order to carry out the program mission and achieve its vision.

As with any business operation, there are key areas in which are grouped the functions that produce the products and services of the business. No different in this situation. Over the program's five-year lifetime, it must develop and make highly effective the functions that will launch the operations that the university and the companies must each carry out in order to achieve the programs mission and vision.

After a couple of hours of work, I called them back into the large meeting room and asked each to identify the key areas. We now had two lists, one from each group with some common items. With some discussion, they were able to combined the two lists into one group of eleven. With further discussion at my urging they were able to reduce the lists down to eight key areas to which the whole team was satisfied. They had identified the functions each key area had to carry out. The team had moved the strategic plan forward and were now acting more like one team. They agreed that at the next month's meeting, I would have the first day. I had moved up in the world!

We continued to implement the steps of the Strategic Way Process on the first day of the two-day session each month. In these monthly meetings that followed not only was a strategic plan developed, a program structure was formed under the operations team, strategic plans were developed and carried out at each key result area level. All of the team task assignments at MIT and within each company necessary to carry out the plans were successfully completed.

The dual Master's degree twenty-four-month program was now in place, attracting the best and brightest students with the majority of the graduates being recruited into the eleven participating companies.

In four years, all of the goals of the five-year program were met in spite of a 6-month late start. Not only that, the operations team declared that they now knew how to implement a Leaders for Manufacturing program at other universities throughout the United States. Ultimately that was the long-range vision and music to my ears.

RESEARCH AND DEVELOPMENT
Investing in the future

Every business needs to consider identifying the functions related to Research and Development (R&D) of the products and services it delivers and to the R&D of the processes that deliver them. In medium and small businesses R&D is so often formally left out of the organization structure. R&D is the strategic lifeblood of any business and does not need to be costly. R&D is at its best when discovered from free sources such as public domain literature. The Internet, the library, universities and the government all are rich with the results of formal research and the experience of others.

Benchmarking of other businesses can provide a wealth of insights. After researching the above sources, it is in the business R&D function that the insights gathered plus any developed internally be fit into the business operation as appropriate. Engage all of the Key Result Areas in the search for insights into how they carry out their functions. Integrate those insights that fit into the operation. Resources need to be allocated to allow this function to take place. It will accelerate the progress toward the business destination.

Lessons Learned: *A vision is not enough.*

THE VISIONARY / MANAGER DUO
A healthy Positive Tension

Visionaries are seeing that which doesn't exist... yet. They have the ability to see the need for a product or service. They see opportunities where others miss it completely. Visionaries are looking outward. They have the energy to seize the moment. Sam Walton thought he could operate a five and dime store better than the current proprietor. He had vision. Steve Jobs saw the need for making computers friendly to use, maybe even fun. Unheard of! The list of visionaries goes on and on. They thrive on discovering something new to produce along with what is being done today. They visualize the need in the market place.

Great managers think differently. They are driven to take an operation and bring it to excellence. They are not satisfied until the products and services are being delivered on time, of highest quality and done with the whole operation running smoothly and using the least amount of resources. They come in every day throughout the year with a smile, ready to accomplish today what was done yesterday only a little bit better. They thrive on turning out the same products and services each and every day.

Now let's put a gifted visionary at the helm without a manager alongside. I have seen this situation in small, medium and large businesses. Their record is often one where the business goes up and down over time. The implementation of new products and services is done at the wrong time or in a most disruptive manner. Where integration of a great idea into the product line is done such that the delivery of current products and services is compromised and the business takes a tumble.

With a most effective manager at the helm the opportunities in their market are often missed. These managers may not see the opportunities because they are focused inward. Even if they see the opportunities they don't want to disturb their smoothly running operation. They often let the world pass them by.

Businesses function best when there is an entrepreneur/ visionary at the helm and an effective manager along- side leading the operation. A desirable positive tension is formed between the two.

Visionaries are swayed by the managers to integrate the new product into the operation in a more orderly manner than they would have done. The managers see the value of the new product, what a great opportunity it is, and give in to bringing it into the operation.

Think of some great companies founded by visionaries with managers alongside. Microsoft with Bill Gates and Steve Ballmer. Steve Jobs with Tim Cook. Go back in time to Harley Davidson and Hewlett Packard. These winning combinations are common knowledge with most, but why these are winning combinations is not so well known.

THE FINANCIAL PLANNER
Entrepreneur and Visionary but not a Manager

Here is an experience with the owner of a small financial planning business that I had engaged to watch over my personal investments.

Greg clearly had the entrepreneurial spirit and was born to sell. Over four years managing the investment of my personal funds we had become good friends although he was achieving poor results with my investments. I told Greg that with great regret I was moving my assets to another financial planner.

Understandably he was disappointed. With his strong desire to grow his company and having a humble heart he asked if I knew how to improve his business. Without hesitating I said yes. That night Greg told his wife that I had fired him and that he had hired me.

I agreed to work with him and his employees using the Strategic Way Process™. In step one, creating a strategic plan was relatively easy because Greg had a clear vision of where he wanted to take the business.

In step two the organization structure is to be optimized. It became clear that Greg was a great marketer and sales person, but did not have the gift or passion for managing the operation. This is often the case. A visionary perceives the need for certain products and services in the market place but lacks the ability to establish an effective operation to deliver those products and services.

We agreed to modify the organization structure to establish a manager position alongside Greg. The manager was to oversee the operation while Greg continued to market, sell and provide overall guidance to the business. This change in organization structure would remove a serious roadblock to moving the operation toward the vision Greg had for the business. We agreed to start looking for a candidate to fill the new position.

Going on to step three, career matching, it became clear that there was no one in his operation that had in-depth experience in developing a high performing financial planning operations. Greg questioned where this kind of help could be obtained. I suggested he attend an up-coming financial planner's conference and seek out a consultant with such qualifications. Greg did just that. The consultant was a partner in a very successful financial planning business that operated outside of Greg's market.

The consultant flew in one evening spending twelve hours the next day assessing the operation. Leaving that evening he promised to send his conclusions in two weeks. Right on time we received a seventeen-page report with specific recommendations that covered every aspect of the operation.

At this point in time Greg agreed with me that it was a good time to fill the newly created manager position. This new manager would implement the recommended changes. He knew of such a person to implement this myriad of changes and to manage the operation long term. He sought out the individual and hired him.

Three years later Greg called me into his office to share what had happened since our application of the Strategic Way Process™. The business had increased assets under management three-fold with more than a threefold increase in profit.

In reflecting on this case study, Greg saw the need for financial planning in the market place. He had a vision for meeting this need. He was successfully attracting people with this need. At the same time, he lacked the knowledge to develop an operation to meet the need and to manage the operation long term. By adding a manager position and then filling it with a competent person resolved the structure issue.

In step three it was recognized that their financial planning expertise was not effective. Rather than hiring a full-time person to bring financial planning expertise to the operation a consultant was brought in for a day. Again, a huge issue was resolved. A valuable lesson is to be learned.

When the workforce lacks expertise in an area of the operation, there are many ways to gain the knowledge needed.

Many times, as I have worked with a wide array of clients there is what I refer to as a "Not Invented Here" syndrome. The belief in the workforce is that they alone are capable of developing all aspects of the operation. Therefore, they are not receptive to seeking outside help. They attempt to grow that expertise from within. It can be a costly task and take a long time to develop. In Greg's case the opposite was true. He was totally open to bringing someone in to inject insight into the collective knowledge of the workforce. And succeed he did.

Applying the Strategic Way Process identified the issues and resolved them effectively. We met for two hours a week over a period of nine months. A minimal time invested to get these dramatic results.

ORGANIZATION STRUCTURE FLATNESS
How many layers

There is a need to address the flatness of an organization when considering organization structure. A blue-chip corporation had thirteen layers in the organization from the executives down to the workers on the floor. To get an approval to spend more than a few hundred thousand dollars it took 6 months. It didn't seem to matter if the expenditure was obviously necessary or not. Because there was urgency for some requests, a Band-Aid was placed on the process. You could quickly get permission with a letter, referred to as a white paper, that would allow beginning to expend the money. And in 6 months the approval would always come through.

A consulting firm came in at one point and worked top management through a process to reduce the number of layers, along with tackling other issues. The outcome was reducing from thirteen to seven layers. The time it now took for the same dollar amount requests to be approved was reduced from 6 months to three days. No longer a need for white papers.

Keep the organization structure as flat as possible and still maintain the oversight needed for the operation. This applies to large and small businesses.

ISSUES WITH MULTI-BUSINESS COMPANIES
Consolidate functions across the businesses or not

Another organization structure issue that arises with a business made up of several product lines is whether to consolidate the common KRA functions required for each product line into one KRA. Examples include marketing, distribution, chip manufacture and many other possibilities. Or establish a marketing KRA, etc. for each business. It is observed both ways have clear pros and cons. The consolidated function across a number of businesses may generate a knowledge base that can be exploited. The consolidated KRA may also lose touch with each of the businesses, become an entity onto itself and poorly serve the individual businesses.

An international corporation had consolidated their manufacturing science and engineering units at their primary manufacturing site. The corporation built a new state of the art manufacturing facility for one of the fundamental components meant to supply several of the company's businesses. The science and engineering group grossly overran their budgets to the point where the unit cost of making product at this site was exorbitant. The businesses refused to use the facility. They preferred to use older manufacturing sites with lower unit costs.

In this same example, its manufacturing site in another country had its own science and engineering unit. This technology unit was continuously commended for serving the manufacturing site and associated business so well, managing costs and delivering the needed science and engineering. The technology unit was physically located next to the manufacturing operation. The manufacturing and technical personnel were on a first name basis. As a result, they had an insight into one another's needs and capability, both focused on achieving significant combined results.

Another international corporation kept its many businesses or product lines quite independent of one another. While I was sitting in a conference room waiting for everyone to arrive for a meeting, the marketing person for that business remarked off-handedly that this particular business within the corporation was considering moving marketing out of the building that contained engineering and the manufacturing operation. The marketing person wondered how they could possibly keep in touch with the business if they were across the street in another building. Interesting.

In a later conversation, the vice president in charge of production in this same corporation was lamenting to me how he had a number of circuit board manufacturing operations that each served its own product line. His concern was that these circuit board operations were not all at the same level of competence. He was debating whether it would be better to consolidate them. And so it goes. No clear direction given here. Seek the consulting firms or universities for counsel.

THE BUSINESS MANAGEMENT TEAM
Horizontal and vertical unity

To assure horizontal interconnectedness of all the areas, the team leader of each KRA along with the business level leaders should form a Business Management Team (BMT). A primary function of this team is to assure all the KRAs form a highly effective operational system. This team fosters an attitude that it is one business; the areas are to be in unity within the business strategic plan and operation.

To assure vertical interconnectedness from top to bottom of the business organization structure:

- Work floor process workers are a team lead by process leaders
- Process leaders are a team lead by task leaders
- Task leaders are a team lead by KRA leaders
- KRA leaders are a team lead by business leaders
- Teams of teams is the concept

- Within each area:
    - Lay out a work flow chart that displays how the functions assigned to the area at business level are carried out within the KRA
    - Identify the tasks, those functions that fit well within a task
    - Within each task identify the processes, step by step, that carry out the function

- At business level:
    - Visionary leader at the helm with an operations manager along side

- KRA leaders with the visionary and operations manager make up the Business Management Team

When businesses describe the work flow in terms of functions, tasks and processes it becomes a source of enlightenment to the workforce and the leadership. In step 6 of the Strategic Way Process the above identified processes will be mapped out in steps that will guide actually carrying out the work of the business.

ORGANIZATION OPTIMIZATION IS COMPLETE
Time to move on

With the identification of the positions that make up the Business Management Team and the above described task and process leader positions noted, the organization structure is now optimized. It is time to move on to step 3 in the Strategic Way Process™ . the career matching of candidates to these positions. The task and process leaders may for the most part be performing in those positions at the time this step is carried out and require no formal matching. It may be necessary to acknowledge that fact when a roll out is done or it may require filling of some of those positions once the business team positions are matched.

Much thoughtful work has been done in implementing step 2. Organization structure optimization is vital to successful implementation of the strategic plan. Do it well and revisit it whenever appropriate. The next step in the Strategic Way Process is to match the right people to the right positions in the organization.

STEP 3–CAREER MATCHED

Right People in Right Positions

The Strategic Way Process Steps:
    Strategically Driven
    Optimally Structured
    Career Matched–You are here
    Strategically Implemented
    Team Operated
    Progress Manage

The career matching step objective is to bring together individual career plans with the functions of each position in the business organization structure. Business leaders have typically suggested all employees are responsible for their own career planning. Yet the leaders typically decide who is offered what positions or which roles to play in the business operation. There appears to be a clear disconnect between these two processes. The career matching process is designed to connect these two processes with openness and integrity.

With the business level strategic plan developed and the organization structure optimized to best support implementing the strategic plan, it is time to put people in positions that best serve them in their career plans and best serve the business in carrying out its mission and achieving its vision.

As a business evolved over time it may have been logical to place a person in a certain position at a specific point in time. It may have made sense for the person's career goals or in the best interests of the business or both. At the present time it may not make sense. To look at the matching of people to the available positions at this time may be just what is needed. The challenge is to initiate a process that addresses both issues and in so doing everyone is satisfied that the right thing has been done. Most leaders are reluctant to touch this challenge except on a case by case basis as the need arises over time. And many times, even then these leaders find it too risky to their careers to do just that.

With the business strategic planning complete and the structure optimized, it is time to put the Core Team to work on the matching process. The Core Team has this proven process to put the right people in the right positions within the organization structure. The team now has the responsibility to carry out this matching process. Read this chapter carefully letting the facilitator guide you through step 3 of the Strategic Way Process™ .

ISSUES TO CONSIDER IN THE
MATCHING PROCESS
Contribution to carrying out the work functions

The central focus of the business leadership in staffing and the associated compensation processes should be heavily weighted toward the value added by each member of the workforce. For a business to have healthy, uncapped growth capability the issue of how much value each individual adds toward carrying out the mission and achieving the vision of the business should be addressed often. For the individual member's career, wellbeing and security in the work place value added is equally important.

When individual value added is high, everybody wins; the business, the members of the workforce, the receiver of the products and services and those who have invested resources.

Another issue in addressing placement of people in the various positions in the organization structure is consideration of how well they fit in the positions defined in the previous step. As I have observed people are naturally wired in very different ways as they carry out work. Some are individual contributors wanting to learn the knowledge and skills to carry out a function and then be left alone to do it whether part of a team or not.

An accountant participating in the matching process shared that until she was shown through this matching process the great appreciation her colleagues had for her work she thought she was not viewed as one who really added value to the business. Prior to the matching process, she thought there was something wrong with her that she wasn't out working with a team but rather preferring to sit quietly in her office. She was a true individual contributor much preferring to work alone.

I have observed that nine out of ten people in most any population seem to be individual contributors whether working alone or in a team. Careers that seem to attract individual contributors in the professional ranks include medical doctors, teachers, attorneys, sale people and accountants. In these occupations they interact with fellow workers but in a dominant role. They are clearly the expert, the most knowledgeable person with support folks gathered around them to assist them in effectively delivering their expert knowledge and skill. Not only in the professional ranks but with carpenters, machine operators, cooks and many more. And for these positions that is most appropriate.

As a result of this desire to contribute individually, it is often difficult to find a manager amongst them. Their interest is not in forming a team of more or less equals and optimizing the operation within which the work is carried out. Individual contributors are focused on getting only the support they need so that they can carry out their role. It seems individual contributors would function without anyone around them if it were effective.

The sales person rolls into the office requesting sales literature, marketing information, etc., gathers it up and quickly moves out to make sales. The medical doctor builds a team around him or her to make patient appointments, keep records, interact with the insurance companies and take vitals of the patient in the examination room. The doctor enters the exam room, diagnoses the health issues and determines the therapy. Everyone in the office is support to his contribution as only he can provide. The doctors typically do not function well as business managers. Why? They are by training or natural selection individual contributors.

Not true with first line managers. I see one in ten in the general population that seem to fit the role of first-line manager or supervisor. They do well when responsible for a team of people carrying out a group of work functions. They effectively assure the team is trained and is producing the products and services intended. They are positively challenged by bringing their total operation to excellence. They develop some kind of system to manage the variables the team encounters. They thrive on increasing the team's ability to handle these various situations. These managers are clearly in contrast to the individual contributors in that they do not deliver the products and services directly but through a team. Although they may do some of the work of the team as well.

Managing a group of first line managers requires added knowledge and skill over the first line manager. I observe that possibly one in fifty seem to naturally make this transition without outside consul. Their success has to do with acquiring the added knowledge and skills required beyond the first line manager. Here is where the Strategic Way Process comes into play. This process addresses the issues present when there are layers of managers. The process is effective whether a business as small as having a few first line managers or having many layers.

This was demonstrated with Dwight owning the financial planning business described in Chapter 5 wherein his small business required but one manger. If you recall Dwight liked to market and sell and was not a skilled manager. He was encouraged to go outside the organization to find a person to fill the manager of mangers role.

Recall in Chapter 4 Mike the plant manager whose business needed to "Make a Buck". He managed department managers. Mike was seeking to make the plant management system function more effectively. Mike was far from being an individual contributor. He sought out someone to bring in the knowledge to deal with the situation he faced. In this case I had the knowledge to address his circumstance.

Many small businesses fail when the transition to manager of managers is required. The owner is an effective first line manager but has not learned the knowledge and skills needed by manager of managers. One in a hundred may naturally be able to manage the managers of managers. These are general observations when considering matching people to positions.

Going through the Strategic Way Process evolving one's management system to a Strategically Optimized Management system allows these positions to be carried out with less innate management ability. The management functions are driven down through the organization structure aiding each manager as will become more obvious as the Strategically Driven Managed System unfolds.

People add value in a wide variety of ways. All are valued as human beings and part of the workforce. The challenge is to put each person in a position to be given the greatest opportunity to add significant value to the business's progress toward the mission and vision. Simultaneously, to personally achieve each person's hearts desire and individual potential.

GOOD OLD BOYS AND NEPOTISM
Demons in management

The business leaders must value how each individual adds value. If business leaders have this value they will want to lay down the good old boys club behavior. I suggest they stop matching people to jobs based on old friendships without priority given to who would make the best fit. A mis-match of capability and position hurts the business. The business is typically using too many resources to get less than best results possible.

Those left out of consideration because of lack of old friendships are deprived of opportunity. It hurts the good old boys as well if they are mismatched because they are not growing in capability nor are they doing what is truly satisfying to them. As tempting as this may be, the leaders need to set aside the good old boys thinking and seek to find those who can best add value for everyone's benefit including the business.

The same applies in putting family members in key positions. For the same reasons placement should be based on fit for the individual and the business not on blood relationship to the leaders.

Leaders are highly effective when they design and operate matching processes in which the business members are creating career plans, using those plans to match their strengths and desires to the work. Where there is no match, the people need to move on to businesses where there is a meaningful match. It may require the individual to gain more training and education, move to another state, etc. Such people need to be encouraged to take the risk, to get out of their comfort zones and seek out a good match.

I personally was strongly encouraged early in my career by the owner of a business where I had been employed for two years to go back to college. When he suggested it in his office I laughed saying I was ready to buy a home and raise a family. He noted that I was naturally inclined to do development work and not production. He stated that I needed more education and credentials. After talking it over with my wife, I went to university earning three majors in science and engineering. It was the best career move I could have made. My only regret was that I never went back to thank him. I share this to encourage the business leaders to take career matching seriously. It is for the good of the business and the employees.

Real satisfaction in the work place comes when one is adding significant value applied to work that is truly important to the individual and the business. Everybody wins!

MATCHING BUSINESS AND KRA LEADERS TO THE POSITIONS
Position needs vs qualifications

As the leaders identify the target or destination of the business through its mission and vision, a key factor in reaching that destination is the staffing of the KRA teams; who does what and how well can they do it. Matching the people with the appropriate strengths and interests to the work is vital. When this matching is done well, a high level of value is being added to every business activity. The work gets done in a minimum of time with the desired results obtained. What then is the effect on the members of the organization?

When workers are able to articulate their career objectives, note and be affirmed of their actual strengths and are matched to the appropriate work there is the potential for them to be motivated to add significant value to the delivery of the products and services of the business. The business is then able to compensate them accordingly for their high level of achievement. The individual is building a larger base of knowledge and skill in their desired work area. They are doing what is most satisfying to them in the work place. If security to provide for themselves and their families is important, and it is to most everyone, there is no better way than to have the capability to add significant value to a business. How then do we accomplish this matching process?

CLARIFY THE ROLES
The Job Descriptions

The business leadership may consist of one over all position or split into two or more positions. In a small to medium sized business, one position may be for overall accountability of the business. Typically, the visionary/owner. A second position is often needed to provide oversight of the whole operation, the operations manager. Other business level positions may be necessary as well. It may include Chief Financial Officer, R&D Director, Production Manager, Chief of Surgery, etc.

At KRA level, one position will be identified for each area. Depending on the size of the business one or more leadership positions may be identified at area level. There may or may not already be job descriptions for the positions to be considered. From the many businesses I have observed it might be well to throw out the job description and start over.

At business and area level the roles need to be documented. It is foundational to describe the roles in terms of what is to be accomplished. To do this, clearly defined objectives are effective in most cases I have encountered. What is to be accomplished in these positions? This would logically include: To development and implement the strategic plan at this level. More specific objectives related to the specific business would be appropriate as well.

In describing the role of the various positions keep in mind the functions the KRA teams have been assigned in Step 2, Structure Optimization. Avoid the how to. Leave that to the individual assigned the position. These objectives are what the individual will seek to meet and will be held accountable to achieve.

Here is an appropriate place for the Core Team to reach out to the Resource Group for counsel as to what the objectives should include. Likewise encourage the candidates to seek understanding of these objectives and to offer enhancements as this process is carried out.

I am reluctant to suggest this be a place to enter goals. Objectives are crafted as long term accomplishments in the person's role. Goals are short term with specific levels of achievement anchored in specific dates. I suggest applying goals on an annual basis with all of the KRA leaders working together as in the "Make a Buck" story described in Chapter 4.

KRA LEADER CANDIDATES
Who are the potential leaders?

The Core Team now needs to identify the candidates for the business leadership and for leading the KRA teams yet to be formed. The Core Team is likely to be familiar with many of these people within the business and some outside of it. This is a good time to reach out to members of the Resource Group to identify candidates. This matching process will likely be an education for the team and the candidates. It typically is an eye opener when the results of the process are reviewed by the members of the business management team who are not members of the Core Team. This matching process is a wonderful expansion of awareness of the capability and career interest of the workforce.

With considerable deliberation, the Core Team should agree upon the candidate list. Expect team members to have differing views about the appropriateness of including some of the considered candidates. Let the matching process sort out the issue with any candidate where there are serious concerns. With Joe's varied success as a leader should he really be considered. That will get flushed out in the matching discussion. Let it happen.

These candidates should be invited to participate in the matching process conveying the understanding that they have been identified as candidates, certainly affirming their ability by being considered, but not assuring that any one of them will fill the identified positions. This will be a great opportunity for the candidates to hear about what attributes they need to possess to be considered in the various positions to be filled. As well, it will give them a new awareness of the interest and capability of their fellow workers.

As a candidate they will provide a resume including career objectives, strengths, experience and formal education. It would be most appropriate for them to read the following in advance to give them perspective in drafting and presenting their resumes.

CANDIDATE PRESENTATIONS
Who are you?

The Core Team is now ready to hear presentations of resumes by each candidate which may well include members of the Core Team. The resume format guides one side of the matching process. The individual candidates for the leadership positions to be filled should have completed their resume.

First, the candidates describe their career objective(s) answering at least these questions: What is my long-term career objective(s)? Where am I along my career path? What am I seeking to accomplish with my career at this time? All else flows from there.

Thinking through the answers to these questions will be a new experience for some. This process will require them to do what is a healthy activity for anyone in the work force. Often significant to the individual and the business is clarification of career direction. Some may express a desire to just do something different. Others may want to gain experience in another area because they are preparing themselves for a higher-level position in the future. Some may have never really liked the position they have held which may be news to their leaders. Many may wish to continue in the position they now fill.

Second on the candidate's resume is a list of the presenters 8 to 10 strengths as perceived by them. These strengths will be enhanced by their associates during their presentation. This is a positive exercise, yet because their associates or peers are engaged, it is a reality check as well. As each strength is noted by the candidate, the peers typically confirm that as a strength. Keep it on the list. Or maybe it's viewed as a more normal attribute to all or maybe even not a strength. In that case, the facilitator should suggest it be taken off the list, all done in a kindly way. Everyone has strengths, but none have all the strengths needed in a business or within a specific team.

Getting back to the presenter, the associates may identify strengths the presenter does not recognize in himself or herself. Add these to the resume list of strengths. Knowing the strengths of each associate is invaluable in the operation of the business.

Third, the resume presenter describes personal work experience by functions carried out, not position titles as titles can be misleading.

Fourth, the presenter notes their formal education. Along with diplomas and degrees they may include the highly valued on-the-job training which so often is the means to their ability to add value to the business.

Looking back at my experiences with the matching process, as people are given the forum for reviewing their past work experiences it helps for the presenters to briefly tell their career stories. They are being heard and appreciated by their peers. They may have never had this opportunity before. I have observed that some have become very emotional for their career history to become known for the first time to their peers.

On the other side of the coin, the colleagues listening to the presenters gain significant appreciation for the people with whom they are working. There is a coming together of these leaders in a new and positive way. Give this matching process the time it deserves. It builds lasting unity in the business.

With each candidate presenting a resume, the other candidates will clearly gain insight into their peers as never before. Something significant happens through these presentations. Individuals finding the right place in the organization structure becomes paramount to all of the candidates. This completes the resume presentations.

MATCHING
Right people to right positions

It is now time for the facilitator to guide the discussion with the candidates for placing the right people in the right positions. The facilitator asks each of the current leaders of the business, starting with the lead position of the business, based upon the presentation of resumes, if they believe they are the right person to fill the position. Here is where openness emerges.

If yes, then the candidates are to affirm it and give supporting commentary. If not, note that as well and explain why. This will most likely be the first time the candidates are given this forum. It should be welcomed and encouraged. It is an opportunity for the candidates to express their passion for the business, their role in it and their credentials to fill the role.

This considered individual may have been on the Core Team through strategic planning and organization optimization and more likely to be comfortable working through this process. This is a clear advantage over the candidates who have not had this exposure to the Strategic Way Process and the Core Team.

With the Core Team and the candidates having been given their input, the leader will either be affirmed in that role or it will be open for other candidates to be considered. Sound dramatic. It typically is not. Informative for all, most definitely.

The remaining candidates should be somewhat relaxed at this point in the process. With the business leader positions filled, the first KRA leader position is targeted. If it is obvious to someone in the room as to who should fill it, they should be encouraged to speak up. Others will likely affirm this person in the position. Someone may offer another candidate. That too should be encouraged and discussed. The facilitator will ask for affirmation by all. Done!

Move on to the next position until all the KRA leader positions are filled. Typically, if you look around the room you will find all are comfortable with what has just transpired. There is unity in the room. Those not select will have other opportunities to fill lower level but equally important roles to play in the business. All will believe that the right people are in the right positions.

Here is an appropriate time for the KRA leaders working together to build their area teams. In most business operations, the KRA's map somewhat similarly to the current organization with some changes made in Step 2 of the Strategic Way Process™ . These changes will have a long-term impact on the progress of the business. Therefore, the workforce within each area will likely continue to perform the same functions as in the past. This means that the workforce within the areas will typically not change dramatically.

But this is the place where obvious changes to personnel across areas should take place. It creates an opportunity for people at this level in the workforce to indicate work preferences different from what they are currently doing. Give them this opportunity to express career preferences, note their strengths, work experience and education with the KRA leaders thoughtfully listening. It may or may not be appropriate to go through the matching process with all area team members. It will depend upon the makeup of the area. I would not expect a mass movement of personnel from area to area, but there will be some who desire change.

With the experience the area leaders have just had they should be prepared to address these issues using the concepts of the matching process if not precisely each step. It will be a breath of fresh air for people within the area to be given the opportunity to consider movement from position to position.

WHERE MATCHING WORKS
A much-needed forum.

The business leader for one of the businesses with which I consulted stopped the process for a period of several months. He finally called me to say he was ready to continue. He addressed the candidates saying that after heading up this business for twenty years he came to grips with the fact that this was never the career he wanted.

He had taken the position when there was a vacuum in terms of available people to fill the business leader position, so he volunteered to accept. It astonished everyone to hear him disclose this fact. So, what did he do? He went off to pursue his life's dream. I hoped at that time that he would live happily ever after. Following up on him four years later, he had gone worldwide with the work he had always wanted to do and was very successful in this new role.

In another case an associate director was responsible for the administrative functions of the business. This role was not being carried out effectively as viewed by his fellow leaders. When going through the matching process he agreed with the objectives that had been identified in this matching process for his current position. When asked if he wanted to continue in that role his response was "That would require an administrator on steroids!" He declined to take on the role. Everyone was relieved. He left the business and became an outstanding mediator. Everybody won!

The leaders of a construction company went through the matching process. The Vice President of Production position was held by Rich for many years. He had held the position as the business grew from small to much larger. During the matching process when his position was considered Rich pointed across the conference room table and said Eric should be in charge of production. Faces around the table showed shock without exception. And yet they all knew he had made the right call. With great concern for Rich they established a landscaping function as part of the business for him to lead. I saw him two years later and asked how he was doing. He said he left the construction company and started his own landscaping business and couldn't be happier.

Another business owner/manager noted in his career objective that he planned to stay in this position for only ten more years. He had other career objectives he wished to pursue. That got everyone's attention. It opened up the possibility of upward mobility for those in the business who had such aspirations.

There is a myth that once in a particular position making changes will create long term issues.

Actually, using a well-designed matching process as describe above will enhance the unity of the organization and demonstrate positive action upon the part of the leaders allowing the mobility to freely move about the organization structure.

Regarding compensation, when matching takes place, there is a broadly understood rule that addresses it quite effectively.

Compensation should follow consistent higher levels of performance with emphasis on consistency.

If sufficient time is given to a higher level of value added, then and only then raise the level of compensation. This allows the movement of people within the organization without needing to immediately reward higher levels of responsibility.

The matching process also fosters movement of people over a variety of positions and work experience. In the case of KRA leader positions, there are some clear benefits to the leaders and to the business to have a particular leader assume leader positions of several KRAs over time or even to take a team member role for a time. This prepares the individual for greater levels of responsibility.

The matching process supports the long-term succession plans of not only the leaders but the whole workforce.

The matching process provides for a deeper bench. Wouldn't you rather have a player that can play four or five positions rather than just third base? Probably the most dramatic experience with the matching process occurred with the engineering division also noted in Chapter 4. Remember the consolidation of all those engineering units and the chaos it created. Initially as we began the Strategic Way Process there was the antithesis of unity. After working through the strategic planning and organization structure optimization the matching process was carried out with great concern for the engineering division and each potential candidate's career. Even I was amazed at the smoothness with which the appointments were made. And the work floor engineers and technicians were all in support of the outcome and relieved with the unity expressed by all the candidates for the leadership placements.

It is not to say that every matching process will have such dramatic results. But the positive outcomes of carrying out the process are remarkably successful in every business where I have observed the matching process used. Those currently in positions and affirming they have been placed appropriately is most encouraging to them as well and everyone in the workforce.

RIGHT PEOPLE IN THE RIGHT POSITIONS
The heart of matching

The challenge: The team makeup that will collectively best carry out the functions of each KRA.

As the Core Team begins to explore this challenge, many "what ifs" need to occur. The Core Team members need to each think outside out of current leadership roles and into some new territory. This will take some encouragement. The team must seriously look at what these area teams need to bring to the table for the area to meet its objectives in carrying out their functions.

It may be effective to send Core Team members off in pairs to research the tasks needed to carry out the functions of each area. Working in pairs allows some freedom from the whole Core Team to research how the area functions are currently being carried out. Time spent with members of the Resource Group may prove fruitful. Looking outside the business by benchmarking other businesses may provide insights. All to come to some conclusions about who should carry out the functions of each area. This research in pairs or individually or with the whole Core Team in meetings is important in placing the right people in the right positions.

What if there are some associates who would better meet their career goals if they left the business? If so, encourage it. What if some work needs to be outsourced? Then pursue it. What if people need to be brought into the business? Go find them.

If everyone should be clarifying their career plans and executing them, then these are valid questions to answer and acted upon for the good of the individuals and for the good of the business. Doing this openly and honestly is the best way.

Answers to the question of what is best for the business and for the individual is the key to really effectively matching people to positions.

The Core Team needs to settle in on the scenario that best addresses the needs of the business and the individuals within it. Most people may be assigned to a KRA team with responsibilities that everyone expected. Some may take responsibilities not expected, but make sense now. Some may have decided to or are encouraged to leave the business for reasons related to their career plan or their lack of fit in the business. Some new people may arrive on the scene. All in the interests of the individuals and the business. There is a challenge to pursue this matching process until the KRA teams are best staffed.

ISSUES TO BE CONSIDERED
Relevant questions to be answered

There are a number of issues to be discussed by the Core Team related to assignments to specific KRA's. Consider each scenario offered by the candidates asking questions such as:

- Do the strengths and experience of the individual lend significant value in carrying out the area functions?
- Does this scenario put individuals in teams that have complementary strengths and experience that will collectively carrying out the functions of each area?
- Do these assignments fit with each individual's career plans in the short and long term?
- Does this scenario allow for a succession of assignments that will continue to carry out the functions of each area and support career plans?
- Are there strengths and experience needed to carry out the functions of the areas that are best satisfied by new hires or outsourcing?

These are some of the issues that need to be addressed by the Core Team and the candidates, yet these are difficult to approach without a process like this–a forum. Keep in mind that all issues should be pursued with two criteria to be met:

1. It is good for the business, that is, it allows the business to carry out the functions of each KRA so that the mission and vision are achieved while minimizing risk.
2. It is good for the individuals; that is, it fits with each individual's career plan.

A particular scenario may not meet these criteria at this time but include an acceptable plan to do so over time. This is a sobering yet freeing experience for all. It puts a positive tension between what is good for the business and good for the individual. It creates a healthy environment for all.

The candidates have had their say, the Core Team has explored the possible scenarios, it is time for the Core Team to decide who will lead the KRA teams and on which of the KRA teams each of the remaining candidates will work. The first to hear of this decision will, of course, be the candidates. There should be time for the Core Team to explain their decisions and to address comments from the candidates. Based upon comments, there may be some changes made at that time if the Core Team agrees. It is certainly appropriate for the Core Team to take the results of the matching process back to the full leadership of the business if they are not part of the Core Team and finally to the business sponsor if appropriate.

Involvement of the candidates in the manner described gives them the sense that the decisions were made with great concern for their careers and for the good of the business. An objective approach was taken with a great deal of input received from the candidates. There is a trust developed here between all who participated that would be difficult to surpass with any other process.

FORMATION OF THE BUSINESS MANAGEMENT TEAM
A natural transition

The leaders at business level along with leaders of each of the KRA teams now quite naturally form the Business Management Team. This team aided by the facilitator, assumes the role of filling out each of the KRA teams with the best match of knowledge and skills needed with that of all the candidates in the business. The use of this matching process depends upon business size and other factors unique to the particular business.

Many of the people at lower levels will more naturally fit into the positions they are currently occupying without need for such a process. The KRA leaders should have the freedom to use the matching process for filling positions within their areas or for just specific positions in their areas. Each leader is now equipped with the awareness of the matching process and its value having participated in the process.

With direct representation of each KRA Team, the Business Management Team will be responsible for general management of the business operation. This team is responsible for assuring that the KRA strategic plans to be developed in the next step of the Strategic Way Process collectively provide the support required to carry out the business level strategic plan. It all fits together on the path to developing a Strategically Optimized Management System™.

The next step is to roll out the work done to date by the Core Team. Those in leadership positions are confident they will be supported by the original candidate list. Those not in leadership positions are satisfied that they were seriously considered and ready to accept their role. The Core Team is confident the right assignments were made.

THE SECOND ROLLOUT
The business organization structure and matching

It is time to rollout the results of optimizing the organization structure to support the strategic plan and matching the right people to the right positions in the organization structure. If the order of rolling out the strategic plan went well, do it the same way. If there are improvements that can be made, do so. Expect that the whole business workforce is now familiar with the format of rollouts and will focus on the new content of this rollout.

Remember to give the business leaders the first opportunity to affirm and enhance the work done to date. Many are on the Core Team, many have participated in the matching process having been briefed on the organization structure. Much of the content to be rolled out is already familiar to them.

For the workforce this will be an eye opener. Again, a breath of fresh air. The objectivity and fairness of the matching process will greatly increase confidence in the leadership. Be sure to briefly describe the matching process. The general conclusion of the whole workforce is most likely to be that the leadership is setting aside any personal agendas and doing what is best for the business.

The workforce participating in the second rollout will be observed, gaining significant ownership in the results. They will be providing meaningful enhancements to consider and owning the results of all this work. To observe this positive response by the workforce is most encouraging to the leadership as well. The workforce is seen as willing to follow the direction laid out by the leadership as never before. See Appendix C for a refresher on rollouts.

When the rollouts to the various audiences are complete and suggested enhancements have been considered and incorporated as appropriate, a transition takes place. The Core Team's tasks have been completed. The business level strategic plan is completed and will now provide guidance for all future work in the business. The organization structure has been optimized. The KRA's have been properly populated with personnel. The leaders and the whole workforce are understanding and owning the results of this work. The KRA leaders are in place and charged with managing the business operation. Core Team, you are out of a job!

THE CORE TEAM CELEBRATION
You've succeeded in your assigned role. Celebrate!

All of this work has been reviewed with the business sponsor and approved. It is time for the sponsor to hold a celebration with the Core Team. Time to eat, drink and be merry. Time to tell stories about the various situations that occurred, some humorous, some very serious, some just interesting. The Core Team may have been on their task for a period of 6 months or a year with weekly or twice a week meeting of two hours each. But the team stayed with it, got the job done and the business stakeholders, that is, the owners, the leaders, the workers are all significantly better for it. It is time to celebrate.

The next step in the Strategic Way Process is the creation of strategic plans for the Key Result Areas (KRAs). These will be developed by the KRA teams in such a way that the business level strategic plan is fully supported. Thank you, Core Team! Now let's get on with the next step.

STEP 4-STRATEGICALLY IMPLEMENTED

Closer to the Production Floor

The Strategic Way Process Steps:
 Strategically Driven
 Optimally Structured
 Career Matched
 Strategically Implemented–You are here
 Team Operated
 Progress Managed

The Core Team has completed the business strategic plan, optimized the organization structure and has now matched people to the work at business level. It is time to shift focus from business level to that within Key Result Area's. The objective of this step is to determine what key strategic part do each of these areas play in the business.

A STRATEGIC PLAN AT AREA LEVEL
Strategically Driven to the Work Floor

A strategic plan needs to be developed for each area guided by the business strategic plan. No better team to do this planning than each of the KRA teams for their individual areas. As each team develops the long-term direction for their area there is clarity established about what they are to accomplish, how it will be done and how to measure progress.

This step in the Strategic Way Process unifies each team while gaining appreciation for the challenges the other KRAs face. Team members within a KRA are looking at the functions assigned to their area. They will be considering how to carry out these functions strategically in a way that supports the business strategic plan.

A KRA strategic plan parallels the business level plan conceptually, only its scope is at area level. A skilled facilitator may be helpful at this level as well in the development of these plans. Often each area team has a Core Team member who can fulfill the facilitation function because of having experienced the process at business level. Or it may be more effective to have a facilitator used at business level planning to guide the process. The strategic plans at KRA level parallel the business plan in terms of components. At business level there is a mission statement and a vision statement. At area level there are a set of objectives and a vision for ideally what these objectives would look like if ideally carried out. At both levels there are strategies and measures of progress.

DETERMINING THE AREA DESTINATION
Objectives and vision

The "Mission" at KRA level is expressed in terms of objectives to not dilute the importance of business mission in the language of the workforce. It would not be constructive to have a business mission and five KRA missions. This is a language issue. The set of objectives at KRA level express what is what is being sought to achieve, the same as the mission at business level. The whole workforce is ultimately seeking to carry out the business mission. But each KRA team has a real mission or set of objectives which they are seeking to carry out in order to support the business mission.

The objective statement format is effective in expressing what a KRA is to accomplish long term. The set of objectives may address specific desired attributes of carrying out the work of the area. KRA objectives normally need to get into a bit more detail than the business mission statement. More specific statements allow the opportunity to clarify what is to be accomplished relative to the several functions assigned to the area.

As will be seen when area progress measures are reviewed, multiple objectives with associated ideal visions for carrying them out lend themselves to developing a powerful measurement system. More objectives versus less is beneficial. Three to five objectives for a KRA are typical.

The ideal vision of meeting the objectives is extremely valuable. As with the business vision statement, the ideal vision of carrying out the work, is something to be sought by everyone in the area. It will provide a picture of what is to be pursued. The format in which this is expressed will be deferred until addressing the KRA measures.

PATH TO THE AREA DESTINATION
KRA strategies

The strategies for meeting the objectives of the area are more detailed than the business strategies. They are guided by the higher-level business strategies, are more specifically steering the tasks and processes of the area and will change as the business strategies change. As new things are learned about carrying out the area functions, the strategies at the area level will likely change. As with business strategies, begin with the strategies that exist today for the area whether documented or not and build on them.

MEASURING PROGRESS ALONG THE WAY
Introducing the Objectives Matrix

KRA measures of progress are directly related to the business measures. Business measures may dictate one or more of the area measures. For example, in a manufacturing plant, unit costs at plant level are an accumulation of department (KRA) costs. There are typically several measures at area level that can be directly added up, so to speak. Units produced in a timeframe for example. For the most part these are obvious measures. There will also be measures unique to the specific area.

The concept is the same as with the measures identified when creating a Business Level strategic plan. If you put the KRA leader in a locked room, what measures of progress would be needed to give a comprehensive view of the state of the area.

An intriguing measurement format is the objectives matrix. It is directly associated with what the area is attempting to accomplish as expressed by the area objectives. It is an objective measure of progress anchored in an ideal vision of meeting an objective. This measurement technique has wide application. A detailed description of objective matrices is in Chapter 9–Progress Managed.

COLLECTIVE SUPPORT OF THE BUSINESS STRATEGIC PLAN
Strategically driven to the work floor

As each KRA team completes a draft of its plan, it is reviewed and enhanced by the Business Management Team. This review is to assure that collectively the area plans carry out the business strategic plan with the highest level of product and service quality, fewest resources used, at the highest potential for success and produced in the shortest period of time.

Once the KRA strategic plans are completed, they become the guidance for laying out the tasks of the area. This will be described in Chapter 8–Team Operated. This concludes the development of the KRA strategic plans.

As you will see in the next chapter, tasks will be assigned within each area team to carry out the functions of that KRA as the way the strategic plan for that KRA is implemented. Within each task, processes are defined and carried out such that the functions are performed in the most effective manner. We will have then taken the business strategic plan and developed it all the way to the work floor. That is the intent of all of this work, to ultimately provide a consistent, comprehensive guide for carrying out the work of the business.

STEP 5-TEAM OPERATED

Teams of Teams

The Strategic Way Process Steps:
    Strategically Driven
    Optimally Structured
    Career Matched
    Strategically Implemented
    Team Operated–You are here
    Progress Managed

The business level destination, that is, the mission and vision, the path to get there, and the means of measuring progress along the way have been defined. The functions of the business to carry out the mission and achieve the vision have been identified and logically grouped as Key Result Areas. The business and KRA leaders have assessed their career objectives and their strengths and have been matched to the appropriate area team creating well-balanced membership. Each area has clear objectives, vision, strategies and measures of progress mirroring the business level format. Much has been accomplished.

The objective of step 5 is to define the operation management approach that will implement the business level strategic plan. Breaking down the tasks within the KRA's to most effectively carry out the work is critical to the implementation of the area strategic plan. In a very real sense, it is time to take the plan to the work floor, into the task by task action required to carry out the strategic plan at area level.

KRA OPERATION TASKS
Breaking the KRA functions into doable tasks

Back in organization structure optimization, Step 2 of the Strategic Way Process™ , business operation functions were grouped into KRAs in a way that the mission and vision of the business can best be achieved. Tasks must now be identified and developed to carry out the functions of each KRA.

This is the time to identify the specific tasks that will carry out the area functions most effectively. In a real sense, this is organization development at area level. The current grouping of the processes that carry out the functions of the area are a beginning. Is there a more effective way to organize the work? Here is a forum for making these kinds of changes to the organization of the work.

Consider the relationship of the processes, communications issues, physical location of the work, flow of the work, etc. One or more people in the area may have long thought the work should be organized differently but there wasn't a forum to express their views. Get the workforce actively thinking "What if..." Who knows the source of innovations? Provide that opportunity now for creativity across the area.

When the dust settles, document the organization of work that has been agreed upon by the area leader with support of the business team. This will lead to definition of the tasks and the functions each task will perform. To ensure these tasks accomplish this, agreements are needed between the leader of each KRA and the task leaders within the area. This is accomplished using a task agreement format. This format addresses the essential elements of an agreement.

Task objectives define what the task is to accomplish. Task outcomes express the visible results of the task processes. Strategies guide how the work will be accomplished. Responsibility and accountability is made clear. The task agreements contain essential information needed to ensure the successful accomplishment of the tasks in alignment with the area strategic plan. A plan to celebrate the successes of the tasks is noted as well. Examples of task agreements are shown in Appendix B.

KRA TASK STAFFING
Allocating staffs within each area

With the tasks thoughtfully defined, the area leader may now facilitate the process to match career plans to task leadership positions. Who can best lead each task and meet their career plans. As with the matching process at business level, do so at area level. Determining what is best for the individual leader candidates and for the area not only put the right people in the right positions but unifies the team as well. The workforce within the areas will believe the right thing was done.

The area leader may also serve as a task leader. The task leaders make up the area leadership team.

Staffing these tasks is best handled as a joint effort between the KRA Team and the task leaders with the support of the Business Management Team, as there may well be negotiations concerning staff and other business resources required.

When the definition of the tasks to implement the area strategic plan is completed, there is clear operations direction with clean lines of responsibility, authority and accountability through which success for all concerned is possible. Give this implementation phase the attention it deserves. Keep the task agreements current and relevant as the KRA strategies evolve and operations staff learn how to better accomplish the tasks. The benefits of all that strategic planning can now be realized.

THE STRATEGICALLY OPTIMIZED MANAGEMENT SYSTEM
The business operation structure – Work floor to the top

Let's walk through the way the business operation structure functions as a Strategically Optimized Management System (SOMS) from the work floor upward.

- Process leaders with a staff of workers carry out each step of each process within a task
- Task leaders are responsible for a group of processes:
  - guided by task agreements
  - accountable to the KRA leadership team
- Area leaders are responsible for a group of tasks
  - guided by area strategic plans
  - accountable to the Business Management Team
- Business Management Team
  - guided by the business level strategic plan
  - Accountable to the next level of management or to the owners of the business

Business level and KRA team leaders make up the Business Management Team guided by the business level strategic plan. Each team is made up of the leaders of the next lower level in the organization structure. All teams are guided by plans that collectively support the plan above. This represents a cohesive management system. From business level strategic plan to task level plans there is continuity, cohesiveness and completeness. This describes the Strategically Optimized Management System™ .

Changes at any level can and should cascade downward or upward as appropriate. Larger as well as smaller businesses with this management systems in place can adjust operations in this manner. Members of one particular large corporation reveled in the fact that the leaders changed a plan at corporate level on a plane while traveling from Hawaii to California. Within days the whole company operation adjusted. In this case it had to do with controlling discretionary expenses based on current company cash flow.

In reality, the Strategic Way Process produces a tightly connected management system that pushes control downward to the lowest level and yet adapts to the guidance from above. Modify a process step and that becomes the method of carrying out that process. Change a task and the processes adjust accordingly, and so on as changes occur anywhere up and down the organization structure. Is this not what leaders desire? Everyone in the structure has the same desire. Let's keep in sync with the direction of the business, be working together, all pulling in the same direction. However, one wishes to express it, this is the power that results from applying the Strategic Way Process which evolves the current management system into a Strategically Optimized Management System™ .

THE THIRD ROLLOUT
The KRA Strategic Plans and Management

The workforce may have viewed the business level strategic plan, the optimized organization structure and the career matching as encouraging but a bit lofty. Rolling out the KRA strategic plans including the tasks that comprise the work of each area and the processes needed to perform the tasks gets much closer to home. There will be strong interest in the content of each area, essentially answering the question: How is this going to function where I work?

Obviously, the Business Management Team (BMT) will orchestrate this rollout. In larger operations, the rollout will be by area to area members. In smaller organizations the rollout of each area may be experienced by the whole workforce. The KRA leaders who are members of the BMT will each present the development work of their area and the area strategic plans, tasks and processes. Taking the management system down to the work floor will be most pleasing to the task leaders, process leaders, and staff.

A favorite professor of mine told his young grandson a story intended to explain the solar system. Illustrating the story with fruit, the professor explained that the grapefruit was the sun, the orange was the earth and the grape was the moon. Grandfather was busy explaining the orbits of the earth and the moon, noting gravity, centrifugal force and how they played out in this system. At one point the grandson interrupted. Examining the orange closely, he asks granddad, "Where does grandma live?"

What is being presented in this third rollout is something like that. Where do I and my process and my work fit in? And that is most appropriate. We all want to know how we fit in. The three rollouts have answered that question from the top down. With the business and KRA leaders familiar with the first two rollouts, there is no need to discuss rollouts further. See Appendix C to be reminded of the details of rollouts.

What remains is for the sponsor of all of this work to again hold a meaningful celebration with the BMT and others who contributed significantly to this effort. Keep it simple, meaningful and informal. Or get more elaborate, if you wish. Just don't escalate celebrations into events that are complicated to plan and carry out. Remember, genius consists of doing things simply but meaningfully.

The next chapter considers how to bring all of the business operation processes to excellence.

STEP 6-PROGRESS MANAGED

Achieving Operations Excellence

The Strategic Way Process Steps:
 Strategically Driven
 Optimally Structured
 Career Matched
 Strategically Implemented
 Team Operated
 Progress Managed–You are here

T he objective of step 6 is to bring both the management and work floor processes to excellence and continually improve them, fundamental to a healthy business. Excellence manifests itself in products and services that consistently meet the needs of the user and require a minimum period of time and resources to produce.

TO ACHIEVE OPERATION EXCELLENCE
Document the work processes, then follow them

And then there is this whole thing of defining, documenting and consistently using the work processes. As noted earlier, businesses may take time to identify and document processes. But the documentation is often done in narrative form, is difficult to modify and becomes out of date. The processes are not then followed. The processes then function out of control. And yet a lack of well managed processes is a barrier to the pursuit of excellence throughout the operation.

In this 6th step of the Strategic Way Process each area team is to break down their functions into processes that provide consistent methods of getting the work done. From the work floor to the highest organization level the processes need to be documented and continuously improved. This is essential to achieving the most effective way of improving the functioning of the whole business.

Some businesses may have documented processes on the work floor but not at higher levels. Most do not have documented processes even at the work floor level. What a missed opportunity for achieving excellence throughout the operation.

We may think of excellence when delivering products and services to the customers of the businesses. What about within the business operation? Recall the work flow diagram described in Chapter 5. Within the operation one Key Result Area's output often is providing input to another area. Excellence demonstrated with this transaction is equally important. Whether a KRA's output is delivered within the operation or to the business customer, bringing the processes to excellence is critical in carrying out the mission and achieving the vision of the business.

In all of this the process operators will experience a high level of ownership in their process when the process documentation is approved and they are in control of their operation and its improvement. All of this leads to high morale.

Out of all of the concepts of Total Quality Management, process documentation is one of the most fundamental. Following documented processes and using the continuous improvement cycle leads to stable, predictable process outcomes which over time lead to achievement of excellence with each of the processes. With stability in the operation, strategies can effectively be developed at task, area and business level to accelerate the operation on the journey toward carrying out the mission and achieving the vision, the destination of the business.

PROCESS DESIGN
Defining the work processes

In the previous chapter, task agreements were made to describe how the functions within a KRA are to be carried out. To do this, task agreements were defined to describe the intent of the tasks, stating why a particular task is done and describing the approach to carrying out the task. Here is where the processes are referenced. The process design is a step by step approach to carrying out the functions that task is assigned.

I would expect most businesses lack a description of how the work is to get done. Where hourly jobs exist, there might be some attempt to define the work, but usually written in narrative form, difficult to read, not kept up to date and simply gathering dust. Professional work is most likely viewed as impractical to describe in any useful way because the work is unique to each situation. So it goes with everything in-between.

The truth is, there is tremendous value in describing the work at all levels including executive positions. It is doable and once understood and experienced, it is embraced by the work force at all levels because of its demonstrated value.

When the knowledge of the operating staff coupled with the added insights of other resources is applied collectively, there is a whole new level of understanding applied to the work. Recall the engineering division situation described in Chapter 4. A top engineer noted "I don't know how to get work done around here anymore." This was a clear case of work processes not defined and documented, in this case, professional work. As engineering units were consolidated, the work processes became muddled. When the engineers sat down and thought through the best approaches to doing the work, documented them and were guided by them, this workforce became highly effective in carrying out its work.

As continuous improvement concepts are applied, the processes can effectively move toward excellence. The products and services become more predictable, of higher quality and require fewer resources to produce. Staff with less knowledge and training are able to get the same high level of results because of well thought out process documentation. The work is done in less time as well. The staff and the recipients of the work gain high levels of confidence in the process and its results. Everybody wins!

PROCESS FORM
Critical to effective documentation

The process design is described in a step-by-step procedure detailing how to do the work. A process form designed in a scientist's laboratory has been adopted by the Strategic Way Process and has proven useful in any area of the operation from top managers to the shop floor. The process form is in table format with a place at the top for the name of the process, the person responsible for the process design and the revision date. The table has 6 columns with each step to be described by a row in the table (see Process Map Form).

Process Map Form

Process: **Process Owner:**

Step No.	Step Description: Describe ten or less steps needed to complete the process.	Step Owner	Step Support	Step Comments: Comments and references here describe how to successfully complete step, shorten completion time and increase quality. Note linkage to other processes here or in By When column.	By When
1				❑ ❑ ❑	
2				❑ ❑ ❑	
3				❑ ❑ ❑	
4				❑ ❑ ❑	
5				❑ ❑ ❑	
6				❑ ❑ ❑	
7				❑ ❑ ❑	
8				❑ ❑ ❑	
9				❑ ❑ ❑	
10				❑ ❑ ❑	

1. Step number
2. Step name
3. Who carries out the step
4. Who supports those who are carrying out the step
5. Bulleted comments noting insights for best carrying out the step
6. When the step needs to be completed

Step 5 is enhanced over time giving highly useful guidance to a new person running the process. Any additional information can be referenced to attached sheets. The whole work process should be described in 10 steps or less which keeps the users maintaining the big picture for that process. For more detail on any one step, reference can be made to sub-processes documented in second layers using the same table format. This table is easy to read, understand and update. Using the form consistently across all work done in the business has the benefit of everyone recognizing the same format for whatever work they are doing from executives to work floor people.

This format has proven effective over a broad spectrum of work from machine operators, to engineering groups, to doctors, to executives of major corporations. Once the work group experiences designing one of their processes and operating from it, the lights go on. The appeal to their desire for consistent, high quality results is innate in people. With this format of the process design in place and consistently used, all are now able to concentrate their effort on the content of the process. On a regular basis the operators have a forum to determine how to improve the process, the area where creativity and uniqueness are necessary and most appropriate.

People will typically not use documented processes on their own initiative. Leaders must lead them through it. Once the processes are designed and used consistently, and they experience the above-mentioned benefits, the battle is almost won. Now the Business Management Team must have the will to see that these formalized processes become habit, that is, an integral part of how work gets done. Now you are there!

THE IMPROVEMENT CYCLE
A cornerstone to achieving excellence

Bringing these processes to excellence involves repeating the improvement cycle over and over. The improvement cycle steps:
1. How has the process performed in the recent past?
2. What changes can we plan to increase performance in the future?
3. Make the planned changes.
4. After the changes are implemented, have the changes produced the intended improvement?

To analyze past performance, the process operators should have data captured to reflect the operation of the process. For example, when were the steps started and finished, was it the right staff, was the documented process followed, were the resources needed available on time, etc. However, the operation was done, did the recipients receive results that met their needs in terms of function, quality, and timeliness or other relevant criteria?

There is an interesting healthy tension that should exist as processes are carried out. On the one hand, take the time needed to carry out each process in a manner that produces a high-quality product or service. On the other hand, complete the process in the shortest time possible. One may take considerable time to achieve high quality and have it not acceptable in terms of timeliness of delivery. One may go through the process steps quickly in order to deliver on time but the resulting quality is poor. This is where the positive tension comes into play. Get the required quality while delivering in the shortest possible time; seek to accomplish both. It is worth the effort to drive both objectives.

Planning process improvement involves learning from the analysis of previous performance of the process, seeking insights from other areas of the business, and looking outside the business by various means. Discussions with associates, doing paper research, benchmarking, etc., all serve to feed the creative ability of the staff as they contemplate changes to the process.

Anyone who suggests ways to improve your processes is helping you succeed. The staff should be strongly encouraged to reach outside of their collective experience to learn better ways of doing their work.

Hands down, the fastest way to improve a process is through the experience of others. Seek it!

Careful and thoughtful implementation of the changes to the process provides the highest probability that the changes will successfully improve performance. Anything less leaves doubt about the value of the changes. Poorly planned and implemented change is a common shortcoming in process improvement. It discourages future change and leaves the process performance less than it could have been. Plan and implement change with excellence.

The objective is to choose designs, staffing and operations approaches to the processes that produce excellence. To do this, there must be an understanding of what changes worked well and to what extent they delivered the desired outcomes. Therefore, the final function in the improvement cycle is assessment of the effect of the changes on the performance of the process. Did we get the results expected? Yes or no and to what extent? Why? When we understand why or why not the changes caused improvement, we are preparing for the next trip through the improvement cycle. We are taking the next step on our path to excellence.

THE MOTOROLA STORY
Product quality is not enough

While working on the MIT Leaders for Manufacturing program, the manager representing Motorola recounted how the company had succeeded in reaching the 6-sigma quality level with manufacture of their cell phones, a major achievement. A high-level Motorola executive went on a tour of customer sites to get a sense for how actual users were experiencing their product. Standing on one customer's loading dock, the dock workers told him how pleased they were with the cell phones. As the executive was walking away, he turned as an afterthought and asked if there were any concerns with the cell phones. One of the dock workers immediately noted that although they really liked the phones it was sometimes thirty days before an order was delivered. The response stunned the executive. He went back to his Motorola office and initiated a task to reduce the processes related to order-to-delivery time.

The task team followed the route from receipt of an order to product in the hands of the customer. For example, at that time when an order was placed with a new customer, there was a credit check that took two days. As they looked at the history of carrying out this step, they found that with orders under a significant dollar amount, the customer's credit was always accepted. Henceforth this step was skipped under that dollar amount. Through diligent effort the delivery time was reduced to less than 24 hours even if it was a custom-built phone while the same high level of quality was maintained. Sales volume increased noticeably. Delivery time does matter for most products and services in any business.

Redesigning the sales order to delivery process resulted in a dramatic reduction in delivery time. This is an example of the importance of managing processes.

THE CONSTRUCTION COMPANY INTERVENTION
An outdated process

I went through the Strategic Way 6-Step Process for a construction company that was very successful building commercial buildings. While putting the plan together the general manager asked if I would take some time apart from strategic planning to look at a serious situation that had arisen in the company's operation. This company had always experienced a full log of work contracts throughout each construction season. They had a reputation throughout the business community for building high quality commercial buildings yet at this moment in time they were experiencing great difficulty in contracting work for the coming season.

The sales people and those putting together the bids for contract were the same people who for years had a record of getting all of the contracts the company could carry out. The general manager had already ordered the layoff of a number of the workforce in preparation for a significant slowdown in work.

I asked that the people involved in the bidding process come together to discuss the problem. I inquired as to what seemed to be the reason that this company was not able to get the contracts. They were in agreement that they were underbid by other contractors. Others could do the job for less money.

I asked if they had changed anything in the bidding process to which they emphatically said no. I then asked why their bid was higher than their competitors. The estimator offered that it was primarily because the competition was willing to build with windows of lower quality, roofs that had lower load strength, etc. I asked, "why don't you do the same thing". He commented "Even though the customer was willing to accept these concessions, this company would not lower its standards. It is these high standards that was a part of acquiring the great reputation that we have."

"Why were these potential clients not willing to pay the price for the high standards of quality." was my next question. The sales people spoke up at this point in the discussion. It was because we were in a recession at that time and the customers needed the buildings but were willing to sacrifice some level of quality. Aha!

The general manger intervened at that point saying, "If we wish to stay in business, we had better make an adjustment in our bidding process. If it means getting enough work for the coming season we needed to offer a lower standard than we are accustomed to delivering. We need to make sure the customers have a full understanding of this change in our standards."

At the close of this meeting as I was walking back to the general manager's office I suggested that all of the company processes be documented and followed. If a problem occurs with any of them at any time, review with the process operators what they are doing. Much can be gained from doing so. He agreed. Within three months the contract log was full for the coming season.

PERFORMANCE FEEDBACK
Essential to high performance

Bringing the processes to excellence through continuous improvement assumes that accurate and timely process performance information is available to the right people in an understandable, timely and useful form. This is what we refer to as performance feedback. It is also assumed that the necessary and only the necessary measures are being used. This is a good time to review two categories of performance measurement.

The most familiar category of performance is often referred to by top level managers as "The bottom line". These measures lag the operation, come after the fact, are the results of having gone through the process cycle. These measures are indicative of how well the process was designed, how appropriate the resources in the process were used and how successful the processes were in delivering the desired results. They are the final test of the health of each process.

The problem with having just the lagging indicators of process performance is that whether acceptable or not, how does one determine why the performance is as it is? If good, why? If not so good, why? The next time the process is run, the results may be different from the previous run. Why?

What is missing are the leading indicators of performance. A set of measures to provide a clue as to why the lagging indicators turned out as they did. These indicators may tell, for example, whether the process started on time, had the appropriate resources been available at the right time, whether the process steps were followed, whether the process documentation was complete, whether the wind was blowing from the west, whatever matters in achieving the desired results.

Here is the real challenge: Do we have the right leading indicators for predicting or correlating with the results expressed by the lagging indicators? This does not just magically happen. It takes thoughtful work over time to nail down the needed leading and lagging indicators that correlate well. It is a challenge that cannot be avoided or ignored. It is needed in the reach for excellence in all of our processes.

To whom, in what format, when, with respect to goals and relationship to celebrations does feedback occur? It is paramount that those who design and operate the process play a major role in the design and delivery of the leading indicator data. These people typically have more insight into and influence over the operation of the process than anyone else. The machine operators or any others up to and including the executives of the business should be expected to exhibit more influence, interest and understanding of the performance of their processes than anyone else.

Therefore, feedback concerning the leading and lagging indicators of process performance must be available to the designers and operators of the processes. It must be timely. Often measurement is done by, posted by and clearly formatted by these people allowing them to pursue their goals while taking corrective action as required. It gives them the ownership and control they need to deliver the desired results. Bottom line or lagging indicators should be of interest to the leaders at higher levels.

THE OBJECTIVES MATRIX
An amazing performance measurement tool

I asked managers in a large firm how they assigned tasks to professionals and how they measured the performance of these professionals. They agreed that cost and schedule were the only really practical measures; no overruns on cost and meeting schedules were pretty much the only measures. These are bottom line, lagging indicators. They noted that the tasks these professionals carried out varied widely with each being quite different. Since these were professional services being rendered there were really no other measures to consider except whether the results were generally satisfactory.

I respectfully disagreed. Had they heard of objective matrices? None had any idea what that meant. I went on to explain that at the outset of a task to be performed would it not be reasonable to state the objectives of carrying out the task, that is, what is to be accomplished? Typically, there may be one to as many as 5 objectives that might be consider. These managers were interested. I offered to describe an objectives matrix. The objectives matrix would clarify what is to be accomplished by the task being assigned. It is not how the objectives will be met, but rather what is to be accomplished.

To design such an objectives matrix, defining up to 5 objectives would clarify what is to be accomplished by carrying out the task. An ideal vision of carrying out the task would allow the task giver and receiver to better understand what is to be accomplished.

With this task, the matrix clarifies the objectives to be met by describing the ideal vision of meeting each objective. Current progress to the vision measures the progress in meeting each objective with a one being just getting started, a five having achieved the vision and a two through four being somewhere in between. The task giver and receiver are to thoroughly discuss the matrix when the task is assigned and as the task progresses toward completion leaving little room for misunderstanding. See the example of an objectives matrix for a task to prepare a facility for medical services use.

Example of an objectives matrix for a task to prepare a facility for medical services use.

Task Objectives	1 Just Getting Started	3 Half Way to the Vision	5 Ideal vision of carrying out the objective.	Score progress to vision
1. To provide a waiting room for patients that meets professional standards.	Found right size room.	Marked door with services offered. Painted walls. Ordered furniture.	Entrance well mark. Room nicely decorated. Greeter professional and friendly.	3
2. To provide exam rooms meeting the medical professional's needs.	Identified needed rooms in building.	Equipment ordered. Rooms decorated.	Each exam room has the necessary equipment for the medical service provider to carry out his/her role.	4
3. To provide office space and equipment.				
4. To ...				
5. To ...				
			Total score	7

The learning that goes on while using the objectives matrix is amazing to observe. The participants are discussing why it went so well or not so well. How they could have done better if...? The task giver begins to better see how the team functions and how he or she could have better stated the task and better clarified the objectives and ideal vision of completing it. The task team has a much clearer target for producing the desired results. As objective matrices are used, in time there is a sharpening of everyone's role.

One can see unity building between the task giver and the task team. You can be assured the next task assigned to this team will be better understood by giver and receiver. The task could be assigned to as few as 1 person or a team.

Objective matrices can be used in a wide variety of situations. They have been used effectively in medical clinics where doctors, nurses and technicians are drawn together by their need to work toward mutual objectives. It has worked wonders in unifying differing levels of knowledge and skill within a team effort that had never been previously experienced or imagined. Similar results have been seen in teams made up of engineers, technicians and maintenance people. When the objectives become common to the whole team, there is a natural desire to make best use of the resources available to meet the objectives.

Coupling the objectives matrix with a task agreement spelling out the expected outcomes, approach to be used, estimated use of resources and schedule for completion there is the high level of getting work done more effectively and with greatly increased unity among all concerned.

Using an objectives matrix does not preclude using some of the more conventional measures of performance. Cost, schedule, units produced, etc., all valid and most often necessary in assessing the performance of a process, task, Key Result Area or business. The collective use of these different types of performance measures is normally the ideal.

GOALS
What people thrive on

At business level, the Step 1 strategic planning measures of performance were established. Let's assume that data was collected over time and a baseline was determined for each measure. As the business leaders relentlessly consider movement toward the destination, that is, carrying out the mission and achieving the vision, it is essential to set some healthy goals that will challenge the entire workforce. In some situations, it may be required for the business's survival, as with the Manufacturing Unit Cost case described in Chapter 4. Remember that "Making a Buck" in a year was the goal. In most any situation, goals can and should provide a healthy stimulus for everyone in the organization.

It is highly effective to carefully set goals at the business level. There then can be a cascading effect to the lower levels. At the next level down in the organization structure, goals would be set to support the achievement of the business level goals and so on down to the work floor. Everyone can now see how reaching their goals contributes to the success of the overall business. This can be a major factor contributing to the unity of the workforce as the business moves toward its destination.

The steps in setting goals are: Determine a baseline, set the goal, note the gap between the baseline and the goal of each measure and identify the logical, doable set of actions that will allow this gap to be closed and assessing the risk of not meeting the goal

At every level of the business there must be responsibility in determining what actions will close the gap. In some cases, the actions are no-brainers. With some there is some risk of being unsuccessful and in some cases this risk is relatively high. All of this needs to be taken into account. The leaders at each level will perform the assessment with insight provided both above and below their levels.

In my experience, working with a wide array of clients, setting smaller goals and meeting them is more productive than setting larger goals and many times falling short. With smaller goals there is a better understanding of the feasibility of reaching them. With smaller goals one would set and achieve them and immediately set the next goals. Smaller or larger goal setting has something to do with personalities too. I will leave that to the psychologists.

A key part of achieving goals over time is to celebrate their achievement. It is not typical in today's western culture to celebrate whether a small enterprise, a large corporation or a nonprofit business. Not so with sports. In sports the goal is quite simple. To win! The players know it, the fans know it, the coaching staff know it and the owners know it. This motivates an entire sports organization to put forth the best possible effort.

Collectively setting meaningful goals against meaningful measures of progress, defining doable gap-closing actions, tracking progress, and having symbolic, enjoyable celebrations make up the recipe for successfully repeating the goal setting cycle over and over again.

It is my observation that people are as much or more interested in the challenge and achievement of the goals and the recognition of their accomplishments by the leaders or colleagues as they are in receiving compensation. Competitive compensation is assumed. Recognition for reaching goals can be amplified by use of symbols such as key chains, baseball caps with appropriate phrases on them, food shared, time off to celebrate, stories told to one another of how the goals were met, all are appreciated by those involved. It works in sports and in the work place.

PART III

TOWARD THE DESTINATION

About Leadership

There are some proven, effective, and straightforward ways leaders can gain the understanding and engagement of the workforce. With significant changes in the business taking place as the steps of the Strategic Way Process are carried out, to be fruitful, the workforce needs to be made aware of and allowed to participate in a manner that is orderly and timely. Leaders can evolve a very positive culture through a number of actions which include rollouts and other techniques noted in Chapter 10.

Chapter 11 speaks to celebrations, a significant tool of leadership. I spent significant time as a middle manager in a large corporation introducing to division and department directors key ways in which celebrations can effectively advance a very positive culture within a business operation. Well defined progress measures combined with meaningful celebrations are what feeds a healthy workplace culture.

Chapter 12 captures some of the insights I gained in my experiences as a manager within a large corporation and my decades of consulting after my early retirement from corporate life.

EFFECTIVE LEADERSHIP

Expecting Results

Over a couple of decades of working with a wide spectrum of businesses one cannot help but gain some insights into excellence in leadership. As you may have observed by now, my interest has always been in achieving results, not theories or generalizations about what sounds like it would be effective. What I have observed about effective management which I believe is generally applicable to most businesses. The objective of this chapter is to share a collection of such observations to which I have been exposed, recurring over and over, in a variety of environments.

THE STRATEGIC WAY PROCESS
Implementation Pace: Keep it reasonable

There may be times when the Strategic Way Process needs to be put on hold for a time. A pause as long as 6 months may be necessary owing to many different circumstances that may arise in the operation of the business. There may be a demand for all resources to focus on the current operation for whatever the reason. Or it may be that time is needed to absorb the changes that have been made up to a point in this process. The key to realizing success is to pause when there is good reason to do so, pick up where you left off when circumstances permit, review where you've been, and then, after the pause, to charge forward.

And finally, the core leadership must be steady and relentless. There will be high points that encourage the leadership. One of these high points occurs when the business level strategic plan is rolled out to all the leaders and then to the total work force. It is an understatement that all will be encouraged by seeing a well-thought-out long range plan for the business. The plan will contain a highly desirable business destination, that is, mission and vision, optimistic, inspiring and worth working toward. It will have clear strategies to get to the destination and actual measures to track progress along the way. Many will never have seen such a thoughtful and comprehensive approach to leadership.

The next rollout will be viewed with equal enthusiasm; a logical, effective organization structure, the appropriate leaders appointed to key positions, and balanced teams built around these key positions. What a breath of fresh air in the business! Prior to this rollout, many in the workforce will have concluded some time ago that the current circumstances will never change for the better.

As the leaders of each of the key result areas develop strategic plans at area level, gain the support of the business leadership, and then roll out their area plans to the workforce, another sense of awe strikes the workforce as they see the continuum of effort on the part of the leadership. The workforce is seeing strategies brought down to the work floor where documented processes are put in place and expected to be used and improved, now all part of their job.

RULE OF THIRDS
An observed phenomenon

Across a business organization, implementation of anything new that is good for the business will typically surface three distinct reactions. This I refer to as the "Rule of Thirds". You may have seen this occur within your business. This will likely occur when the Strategic Way Process is carried out. As the leaders move through the 6 steps, as with anything new that has been launched, one-third will hardly be able to keep their feet on the ground as they see the value of what they are being exposed.

They will see the benefits to the business and will be most enthusiastic. They will be ready and willing to think through all the issues that must be addressed. This group will aggressively seek to identify and implement the changes that come out of the Strategic Way Process™ . The leaders will eagerly seek the nod to communicate the changes to their people. This first third will be ready to put the changes into practice as soon as the rest of the leadership will permit it.

There will be a second third that will just not be sure these management changes are the right thing to do. They need more time than the first third to discern the true value of the changes and the possible unintended results of the changes. They could be characterized as cautious. They are not less capable, they just take a more deliberate approach to the new and different.

This middle third is not at all sure of what it is that is being introduced and whether it will benefit them, and they do little to embrace it until the first third has achieved some obvious success. At that point, they will implement, but certainly in a more paced manner. They complement the first group in that they rightfully slow down the process a bit, not stop it, but cause it to just proceed at a bit slower pace. A positive tension between these two groups is normal and healthy.

The third group, which thrives on independence, will see these changes as an assault on their control of the environment for which they are responsible. They have a stronger sense of independence than either of the first two groups. These leaders tend to be close to their own workers, do well in performing their work, are proud of their accomplishments and are somewhat inward focused. Change from the outside is not particularly welcomed. They are loyal to their own and to the business, but just not so tightly linked to the overall business. In the end, as they see the value in something good that's introduced to them, they will be some of the strongest proponents.

These three groups are observed at all levels of employment. The rule of thirds occurs with the full spectrum of job types from executive to middle managers, to administrative assistants and machine operators with amazing consistency. It is somehow put into the design of people by our maker, therefore it must be for the good of us all. To be aware of this response makes more effective change strategies possible. When there is something good for the business to implement, clearly and concisely present the What, Why and How.

Going through the Strategic Way Process plays out well with the three groups. As leaders commit to carrying out this process at business level, the first third will be the driving force that carries out the process. When obvious positive results occur in developing the strategic plan, there will be enough momentum to move on to organization structure optimization. With the positive changes occurring at this step, there will now be enough confidence on the part of all three groups to continue through the remaining steps.

Especially interesting is the obvious energy of the third group when step 4 strategic plans are developed for each KRA. This third group will have experienced a positive result with the business strategic plan, so these people are eager to do plans for their area. They have also experienced the unity and support of the whole leadership of the business as they proceed through the process steps. And of course, they wouldn't want to be left behind at this stage of the game.

The important point of this phenomenon is to recognize the existence of the three groups, and know that their reactions to change are normal and that all three groups actually allow for successful implementation, each reacting in their own way, to the overall process. The first 3 steps of the Strategic Way Process give the first third the opportunity to be first to implement, the second third the chance to observe the success of the first group, and the third group the opportunity to isolate a bit and do their implementation when ready. It all works out.

INTRINSIC VS EXTRINSIC CONSEQUENCES
Both are useful, one is preferred

Whether we are conscious of them or not, there are consequences to every action.

A well-known consequence is punishment. Putting one's hand on a hot coal has an immediate negative consequence, punishment via pain. This consequence stops the behavior that caused the pain. The consequence of punishment can be delivered deliberately by a parent whose child runs into the street or a supervisor who sees an operator acting in an unsafe way. We are all experienced in receiving and delivering punishment.

A second consequence was labeled negative reinforcement by Dr. Aubrey Daniels in his book *Performance Management* (p 28-31).[1]

> "These (negative reinforcements) are consequences to behaviors that people will work hard to avoid. If we have a toothache, we will go to the dentist to get rid of (escape) the pain... Putting on safety glasses to avoid getting chewed out by the supervisor... In a work environment that is managed primarily by negative reinforcement, people will do what they must to avoid negative consequences."

---

[1] PERFORMANCE MANAGEMENT
Improving Quality Productivity through Positive Reinforcement
Third Edition, Revised
Aubrey C. Daniels, Ph. D.
Performance Management Publications
Tucker, Georgia

Punishment and negative reinforcement are consequences that impede undesired behavior. Negative consequences are best kept to a minimum in the workplace.

A third consequence, according to Dr. Daniels, is extinction.

"When people do something and as a result get no reinforcement, positive or negative, they will be less likely to repeat that behavior in the future... A frequent problem in many work places is that productive behavior is ignored. The people who work the hardest and do the best are ignored because the supervisors are spending all their time dealing with the problem performers."

Unlike dealing with small children, extinction is practiced far too often in the workplace. When the toddler is learning to walk we quite naturally heap praise on the child when that wobbly first step is taken, and continue to do so until the child is walking routinely. Adults can be thought of as taller children in that we all covet praise or positive reinforcement. We all want to be recognized for our accomplishments.

The fourth consequence is positive reinforcement. Positive reinforcement is by far the preferred and most effective reinforcement to use in essentially every situation.

"...provide positive consequences for desired behavior for the purpose of increasing its frequency or intensity."

Awareness of these consequences and the effective delivery of them in the workplace can bring about highly desirable results for the entire workforce. This applies to all levels of the organization. A thumbs up, a smile, a little celebration when something of significance is achieved, can make a big difference in whether someone on the work floor or a leader continues to strive for high performance. Inadvertently triggering inappropriate consequences will tend to reduce performance.

There are two ways to deliver consequences. When someone observes a behavior and delivers a planned or unplanned appropriate consequence this is referred to as an extrinsic consequence. It is initiated when someone's behavior requires observation or intervention. Celebrations planned for completing a task, meeting a goal or achieving some extraordinary result, are examples of delivering positive, extrinsic consequences. This requires one or more persons recognizing the reason for the celebration and delivering the consequence.

In contrast, intrinsic consequences are built into the action or behavior, that is, the consequence is delivered without outside help. Whenever consequences can be built into an activity, significant value can result. In the design of processes, look for opportunities to do so.

The Core Team completes the task of developing a strategic plan. The sponsor and the business's leader throw a little celebration party; this is an example of an extrinsic consequence. A process is designed in such a way that when the operating staff start on time, carry out each step as required, the results are of high quality and delivered on time with minimum resources expended; this is an example of an intrinsic consequence. They observe the results of their good work.

Effectively designed activities with built in intrinsic consequences for those who carry out the activities are most desirable. No intervention by an outside source is needed.

COMMUNICATIONS
Manage it well

There are several criteria to be met when addressing communications. It is necessary to identify the sources of the ideas and events and such that are to be communicated. Determine where this information is to be directed, that is, decide who needs to receive it. Thoughtfully design the format in which this information is to be communicated. Clarify the value of communicating this information. Regularly test the effectiveness of the communications. Consolidate the system of communication within and external to the business so that the communications meet everyone's needs using a minimum of resources.

To meet all of the fore mentioned criteria may seem like a tall order. It is! It is also essential to the healthy operation of a business. A well-thought-out communications task agreement provides assurance that a more strategic approach is being taken to this function. Processes that are thought through and brought to excellence allow the communication function to generate consistent and predictable results. Staffing the process with people gifted in communications knowledge and skill assures continued commitment and passion for the task. With a task agreement, clear processes and the right staff in place, effective communication becomes a reality.

There are a few things the communications group needs to keep in mind. It is necessary to coordinate communication of information to ensure consistency of thinking across the groups within the business. Communicate topics repeatedly to allow them to sink in to the people's minds and being.

Use written, verbal, graphic, dramatic, and symbolic venues, in short, use all available means to effectively address the way people learn and retain ideas and concepts. Seize opportunities to engage people in active participation when communicating with them. For example, rollouts engage them when they are asked to feedback affirmations and enhancements to information presented to them. This is done in small groups to allow everyone the opportunity to become actively involved. Effective communication is an essential part of a successful business. Value it!

CELEBRATIONS

Real Need–Small Cost

I magine a business where co-workers recognize when someone accomplishes something of value and gives the person a compliment, round of applause, slap on the back or words such as *good job, way to go, great effort*. Then take it a step further and see little celebrations of coffee and pastries or hand out of a certificate of appreciation made up on a personal computer. And on occasion where the initiative is taken to invite an individual or team out for lunch or provide tickets to some special event. Where there is an atmosphere where people are trying to catch associates doing something right and letting them know that their efforts are appreciated. This is characteristic of a healthy business. The objective of this chapter is to share how to achieve this atmosphere throughout the business.

SO LITTLE EFFORT, SUCH GREAT REWARDS
It's a natural part of life

To achieve this healthy atmosphere requires intentional positive feedback to individuals performing small as well as significant tasks that help carry out the mission and achieve the vision of the business. Such compliments, rewards or celebrations are actually extrinsically delivered positive reinforcements.

Likewise, work systems designed to include the opportunity for participants to receive a sense of accomplishment and satisfaction are referred to as intrinsically-delivered positive reinforcement. Both extrinsic and intrinsic reinforcement should be experienced by the work-force to facilitate the achievement of the highest level of excellence.

Delivery of positive reinforcement for maximum impact should follow a few important guidelines. The specific achievement should be stated, and the one delivering the reward should be sincere in expressing personal gratitude. The reward should be given immediately after the achievement occurs and it should be of value to the recipient. Remember: Specific, Sincere, Immediate & Personal (SSIP).

What follows are some noteworthy celebration stories intended to bring joy to the work place in reward for work well done.

THE GRUFF CEO
It took courage and a bit of belief

The CEO of a blue-chip company was known for being gruff and demanding. He would often set dates for budget submissions that were unreasonable and difficult to meet. He seemed indifferent to the hardship this practice caused many managers throughout the corporation. When the budgets did get turned in on time and in acceptable condition, the CEO would not acknowledge the hard work and long hours spent by his subordinates in getting the task done on time.

One of the CEO's general managers had attended a course on performance management. The course stressed the tremendous benefits of positive reinforcement following the performance of good work. One day after the CEO had just set another unreasonable date for task completion, the general manager saw the CEO in the hallway and thanked him for giving him a reasonable amount of time to get the task done. He commented that it made the task so much more enjoyable for his direct reports to do the work. The fact was that no more time than normal was provided.

The CEO seemed to hardly notice the comment, but the next day he sent out a memo noting how much he appreciated the hard work and timeliness in which they all completed their tasks. In the ensuing year the CEO seemed to have changed the way he set expectations for his general managers. He now seemed more interested in what made their work enjoyable. All of this stemmed from a single comment made in the hallway by a general manager to the CEO.

Obviously, the CEO was receptive to positive reinforcement even when it was unwarranted. The general manager continued to provide positive reinforcement to the CEO, but now only when it was warranted. The relationship between the CEO and all of his general managers improved greatly as time passed. The CEO softened a bit in tone as well, becoming more of a colleague than a dictator. All of this began with one of his direct reports letting him experience some positive reinforcement.

THE SECRETARY'S LUNCH
Not my cup of tea

The director of research always took her secretary out for lunch at the end of the year to show appreciation for the secretary's excellent performance. One day one of the division directors asked the secretary how she felt about the annual lunch date. Without hesitating the secretary said she really liked working for the director but she found the lunch punishing because she had nothing in common with the director and would much prefer something else such as a gift card for a pedicure.

The division director relayed this to the research director. The director was very much into science and research, had never had a pedicure, and simply could not relate to this form of positive reinforcement. She continued to take her secretary out for lunch; some people just don't get it.

The research director is not alone in thinking that what is positively reinforcing to them would also be reinforcing to someone she would want to encourage. Take the time to find out what is liked or pleasing to the intended recipient of positive reinforcement and deliver that, thus accomplishing what you intended.

Sometimes something as simple as handing out baseball caps with the task or program name on it at the end of the effort is most effective. Why do people value little statues of someone swinging a bat or holding a golf club in the backswing position? These tokens are symbolic of accomplishments. Money or other compensation often is not necessary. Effective encouragement and recognition can come from something as simple as a gesture, a thumbs-up in passing by.

HAM-N-REDEYE GRAVY DAY
The whole workforce engaged

The managers of a major division of a company in the south were challenged to increase sales to adequately fill the manufacturing capacity of the plant site so as to reduce unit cost to a level that would generate acceptable profit. The manager wanted to engage the entire workforce in meeting this challenge.

The goal to be met in the current year, stated in sales revenue, was announced by the manager in January, suggesting that in some way everyone could contribute to the sales goal that would sufficiently fill the plant capacity. If the goal was met, the whole plant would celebrate with a ham-n-redeye gravy party with all the trimmings on the plant lawn. Ham-n-Redeye gravy was a coveted "thing" in this southern locale. Everyone began to take personal actions with, of course, the sales force working all-out and thinking of ways to sell more product. Some office jobs were streamlined to release personnel for sales support work. Marketing was developing innovative ways to present the products to clients. Engineering and maintenance initiated activities to make manufacturing more efficient. The credit union figured out ways to keep the lines short so that workers could get back to their jobs.

In April as sales increased, the general manager announced that the ham had been bought. There were smiles evident everywhere of the encouragement to keep pushing. Everyone was energized to do whatever they could to influence reaching the goal. In July as sales grew even more, the general manager said the ham was in the oven. Work continued at an even more intense rate by everyone to reach the goal.

On a day in November the sales goal was reached. Management declared "Gravy Day". The celebration began at noon for the whole workforce. Ham n redeye gravy with all the trimming was served on the company lawn. The general manager noted how important meeting this goal was to him personally and to the company. Everyone beamed and enjoyed the ham n redeye gravy and a half day off to party.

Management encouraged the telling of stories by many different workers describing how they had contributed to reaching the goal. The party ended at the close of the afternoon with everyone feeling good about meeting the challenge and feeling good about themselves and each other. They enjoyed their ham n redeye gravy dish, an afternoon taken off from work to celebrate with no additional compensation involved.

Engaging people in the performance challenges of the business with planned recognition upon success enriches the workplace environment.

Leaders take note. Yes, it takes time to create something meaningful for the workers, but doing so is always worth it.

REFLECTIONS

The Experience

The Strategic Way Process addresses major issues every business operation encounters. For any one business there may be only a few issues that need attention. If the business is satisfactorily carrying out its mission and moving at an acceptable pace toward its vision than this process could be viewed as an audit. If all the stakeholders are satisfied with the performance of the business than the only concern would be to maintain or exceed that level of performance. The reference to stakeholders includes the receivers of the products and services, people that produce them, the governance of the business and the owners.

If all of this were true however, how would any one stakeholder know that all is well. Herein comes the concept of auditing to assure everyone that all is well. In my years of consulting I have yet to encounter a business that did not benefit from walking through the 6 steps of the Strategic Way Process annually. Most common is to observe significant benefit from carrying out each step. Some steps will be more helpful than others for any specific business. Though most profit from each and every step done annually.

THE 6 STEP PROCESS
First time vs following years

Typically, the first time through the 6 steps takes by far the most time. Two things are happening. All are learning how to apply the steps and the content is being generated and documented for reference and communication across the business. Undocumented content is easily forgotten over a period of time. The following year when the 6 steps are carried out again, the time will be largely devoted to modifying content from the previous year based on what was learned over the past year and changes in the internal and external business environment. Therefore, significantly less time will be required.

Walking through the 6 steps, there now is complete strategic plans with solid grounding in our current situation, well thought out mission statements and inspiring ideal visions of carrying out the functions of the business. There may also be an inspiring slogan capturing the above in a few words like "Team Xerox". Meaningful values are being propagated across the work force encouraging a positive shift in the culture. There are effective strategies developed, documented and ready to be tested for viability. And there are minimal yet comprehensive leading and lagging measures defined to mark progress toward the mission and vision.

Organization structures are optimized for plan implementation. The current structure has been scrutinized for what is best to carry out the strategic plan with changes made accordingly.

The right people are matched to the right positions giving everyone the sense that the right thing has been done in allocation of the workforce to the operation.

Lower level strategic plans have been developed, most likely for the first time, to help breakdown the business strategic plan into a more understandable form to implement.

The team approach to organizing the work is either reinforced or done for the first time allowing more effective execution of the work and providing a richer environment for all to work within.

And Total Quality Management concepts are being implemented vertically and horizontally across the organization allowing all processes to be brought under control and then to excellence.

In all of this, there have been timely rollouts of the content developed in the Strategic Way Process™. In Step 1, the business level strategic plan was rolled out to the workforce at several levels. Again, there was a rollout to present the results of both Step 2 Organization Structure Optimization and Step 3 Career Matching and finally at the end of Step 4 when Key Result Area strategic plans were rolled out.

The rollouts have a wonderful way of communicating the organization development work done, engaging the workforce through presentation, affirmation and enhancement of the work. Everyone now knows what is going on and why and of equal importance, they have had an opportunity to influence this work where significant contributions are typically made.

Because the workforce was engaged in the rollouts in this manner, they tend to take strong ownership of the work done using the 6 steps. This will have a significant impact on making these changes effective. Every decision at every level will be moving the business toward the same destination, that is, to carry out the mission and achieve the vision. Who could ask for more.

THE MEDICAL SERVICES CENTER
Off Mission

The newly appointed director of a non-profit medical services center sought out my expertise in developing an effective management system for the center. Jim indicated that in his recent appointment as director he had become deeply concerned about the management of the operation. Jim readily confessed that he had little experience in management but had a deep conviction that it was important that this center get back on mission. He noted that in his assessment, this center and others like it across the country were off mission as well.

He felt compelled to return this medical center to the mission they were founded upon. He had tapped into many experts in the medical field as well as other areas of expertise relevant to his center's successful operation. He was receiving great insights from these experts. They had demonstrated an obvious willingness to serve this non-profit business. Jim asked if I would be willing to give of my knowledge in building an effective management system.

Agreeing to do so we assembled his management team and began walking through the 6 steps of the Strategic Way Process™. As I guided the process, they began to accurately assess the current medical center operation. They then crafted a mission and cast a very compelling vision of carrying it out. The mission and vision became the new medical center destination, far different than the current road they were on.

Identifying relevant values was done to shift the cultural thinking of not only the management team but also the host of volunteers and donors supporting this non-profit business. Embracing these values was to shape their internal culture, thus, increasing the potential of reaching the destination of the center.

Then they wrestled with the strategies (approaches) they would use to reach the medical center mission and vision. The strategies continue to be modified today as the environment changes and they learn about what most effectively moves them toward the destination.

Progress measures were struggled with for some time. With great tenacity on the part of the leaders the measures began to give the managers, medical staff and the volunteers, the performance insights they needed to guide their actions. As these measures evolved, the progress was not only inspiring to them but showed them what approaches moved the business on this journey toward the destination and what did not.

Today they are using a highly-refined set of progress measures. The data is collected on a cloud system and fed back in real time to those that need it. Never underestimate the ability of a non-profit to perform with excellence right up there with businesses that are pursuing a profit.

What drives leaders and the workforce as much or more often than a profit motive is the pursuit of their vision for the business.

This medical services center had gone from performing off mission and at a poor to mediocre level of operation to a top performer in their area of medical service. Not because of the Strategic Way Process but with it along with many other insights brought to bear through people with specifically held expertise. A significant role in their success was the thoughtful, persistent effort of Jim, their director. Their vision drove these people, engaging the leaders, the volunteers and the experts. In this business, none of their effort was for a profit. All was to carry out the mission and achieve the vision for the center that Jim and his leaders had so thoughtfully crafted.

STRATEGICALLY OPTIMIZED MANAGEMENT SYSTEM (SOMS)
Can be transferred

Is it possible for any business to transfer their specific Strategically Optimized Management System to multiple locations or to other organizations in the same business? I don't know why not. I personally have seen this done with the medical services center described in this chapter. A successful transition does seem worthy of consideration.

Was the Leaders for Manufacturing program at MIT able to transfer their model to other universities each with their unique set of associated companies? That was in the vision of the Leaders Program at MIT. This would scale up the impact on United States manufacturing being obtained with the MIT program. With some variation of the Leaders Program most of the design under the discipline of the Strategically Optimized Management System could most certainly be transferred. The vision of the MIT Leaders Program would then be and was achieved.

The discipline within the design of a Strategically Optimized Management System creates a platform for making possible these transfers of model operations. This is the basis of most franchise operations. Each franchise then has the opportunity to have all of the positive characteristics of a Strategically Optimized Management System^{TM}. There is no limit to the possibilities.

Those familiar with the concept of benchmarking would see the potential for more effective transfer of insights and methods as well. The term, benchmarking, comes from the shoemaker's shop of old where the proprietor would note one of his craftsman who did outstanding work on say, the application of the heel to the shoe. The proprietor would then gather the other craftsman around this bench and have them learn from the techniques the expert heel applier was using. The concept is simple and effective providing a step function improvement in the shoe making shop.

Businesses for years have applied this benchmarking concept in learning from non-competing businesses with outstanding performance in a particular work flow function or work method. A business that excels in warehouse distribution could offer their methods to non-competing businesses needing to improve their warehouse distribution operation with the two in non-competing markets or products and services. In return the receiving business would share insights related to an expertise they had acquired.

All this to say to business leaders who have evolved their management system to a Strategically Optimized Management System™, the opportunity to effectively do benchmarking is greatly enhanced. We are now addressing not just workflow methods but the whole management system for that function. A way to greatly enhance the benchmarking concept.

A CLIENT BUSINESS SYSTEM TRANSFER
Medical Services Center story continued

Here is an example of an actual transfer of a Strategically Optimized Management System (SOMS). Earlier in this chapter, there was a non-profit Medical Services Center that had gotten off mission. As described, this center with the aid of a number of experts in various fields had applied their knowledge to this center operation. The center leadership had gone through the Strategic Way Process three years in a row.

The success in progressing toward their mission and vision for their business was so outstanding this center was approached by three similar medical centers who were off mission, one on the east coast, one in the west and one in the south. These centers wanted to know how such success was achieved and could they learn the secret to this center's success.

This center had a mission and vision that fit well with the directors of these inquiring centers. Through the Strategic Way Process all of the key parts of this center's Strategically Optimized Management System were documented from mission and vision to strategies and all the way through to every process being documented, actually used and continuously improved. Why not consider training the inquiring centers for they were not competing in this center's market location. The center director, Jim, had the same heart for people's medical needs being met elsewhere as in his own location.

After some thoughtful discussion with the three center directors and his own staff, the strategy would be to share Jim's strategic plan with directors of these centers, gain their understanding and ask them to each gain the same understanding with their center's governing board. Jim mentored them as they plowed through his strategic plan.

The lights went on. Each in their own time began to see the thinking documented in Jim's center plan. Jim spent significant time with them to assure that each director had a clear understanding of his center's plan and assurance that each center's board had sufficient understanding to support implementation of the plan.

At this point Jim and some of his staff members began to roll out the organization structure they had optimized to support the plan. This was followed by explaining and assuring that the leaders of these three centers understood and could implement the matching of people to KRA positions and so on through the 6 steps of the Strategic Way Process™ . This required Jim spending time mentoring the directors through each step allowing for uniqueness as required for each of the three centers. Where Jim's center content could be directly transferred to the three centers it was done. Where not, Jim guided them through the specific step. Believe me, this book would have helped at the time. Jim will testify to that.

A situation where these three centers could benefit greatly was in receiving Jim's strategic plan and organization structure verbatim. Likewise, with the processes to carry out the functions of the Key Result Areas. It was a huge step function change for these three centers as this represented three years of development at Jim's center. Portions of the rest of Jim's management system were also transferred as appropriate.

Within nine months of completion of the transfer to these three centers they were performing at the same level as Jim's center. Quite amazing! They had been performing similar to where Jim's center had been three years earlier. Now other centers were inquiring of these three centers as to how they were getting such remarkable performance. This was fed back to Jim. At this point he made a most ingenious move. He suggested to the three center directors that they take on the role of training the inquiring centers that would be willing to make the transition. Their enthusiasm was so great that they did just that. It resulted in similar step function gains by those centers that chose to make the change to the model Jim had developed.

Jim has gone on to develop his center's performance feedback system on cloud software. The centers to which his model has been transferred have been integrated into his performance feedback system. Feedback is now instantly available to all of the participating centers. Impressive!

I can think of many business situations where transfer of a successful operation to other sites would be highly valuable. The new sites benefit from most of the development work done by the first site. It dramatically reduces time required to get to the model site's performance level and essentially eliminates much of the development time and costs. Something to consider by many businesses.

THE CLIENT STORIES
What they demonstrate

These five distinctly different businesses had situations that were unique to each of their operations. The issues blocking the leader's journey toward their visions were significant. In these stories, the leaders had not been able to resolve the issues until the point in time when they embraced the Strategic Way Process™ . As a consultant, I knew little if anything about their business operations. Yet by merely guiding the leaders through the 6 step Strategic Way Process the unique issues each had were resolved.

Their issues were resolved as these leaders began to evolve their current management system into a Strategically Optimized Management System (SOMS™). The SOMS has been demonstrated to be highly effective not only in these five cases described above, but with every business that I have worked with that embraced the 6 steps of the Strategic Way Process™ .

Of the client stories I have shared I have purposely not identified the businesses by name or given any specifics that would do so. Reason being that I want the reader to focus on the Strategic Way Process and not get sidetracked by the specifics of any one business.

I should caution that high levels of success have not been achieved when business leaders half-heartedly apply the 6 step Strategic Way Process™ . They might get some positive results part way through the 6 steps and then are satisfied with that limited success. They may go through all 6 steps but for only one cycle not repeating the cycle each year. As a result, the evolution toward a SOMS is halted.

A SOMS evolves over time. Great gains are typically made in the first cycle through the 6-step process. Continuing gains will be made as the cycle is repeated annually.

The message: Stay with the process!

MIT SLOAN SCHOOL OF MANAGEMENT WORKSHOPS
Masters level students demand publishing

While working on the Leader's program at MIT and seeing the effectiveness of the Strategic Way Process on this five year program, I was invited by the professor of strategic planning at the MIT Sloan Management School to teach portions of the process annually to two masters level degree programs, one for students coming directly out of an undergraduate science or engineering program and the other class with students with at least five years of work experience prior to entering the master's program.

The professor would block together two one-and-a-half-hour class sessions and add an hour totaling a four-hour block scheduled from four to eight PM on one of the days I was working on the Leader's program. I would spend the first half hour lecturing on some aspect of the Strategic Way Process™ . I would then form teams of four students each. I would ask each team to apply what I had presented to some imagined or real business at their discretion.

Each four-person team would then come back to the classroom and present in four minutes the results of their efforts to the rest of the class. Each group applying the concepts I had presented and then seeing how other groups applied the same concepts. This show and tell was a great way to help them to see the power of the concepts. I was amazed at how quickly they picked up on the portion of the process covered in the half hour lecture. The last half hour of the four-hour session was a Q&A segment. Each class was always really energized by this four-hour workshop.

Through this experience the students could visualize how the concepts could be used in their field of work to improve whatever management system within which they were now or would be a part of. The only complaint I received was that the whole process was not published. Some became very upset. They wanted to take the process back to their workplace when they graduated. Well, I finally got to it–this book. I hope they will forgive the delay.

IN CLOSING
Reflections

As business leaders complete the first time through the 6 steps of the Strategic Way Model there typically is a deep sense of satisfaction. There was a great deal of ground covered related to the business. The leaders, especially those on the Core Team, were able to express views about the business that had never before been given. Maybe there wasn't the appropriate venue for doing so. Often it could be the 6-step process that prompted thoughts in a particular area. Or other team members expressed views that were an encouragement to all on the team to react to in support of or to build on a view. Or to point out the shortcomings of that particular view so that together the team could discard it.

In any case, the Core team members, with a facilitator guiding the process, had the opportunity to freely discuss, in a safe environment, the ideas that were coming to mind. It was an opportunity to explore a wide range of concepts to consider for the business. The team could build on ideas or with discussion, determine they are not for this business.

As work was completed, the 6-step process led to the Core Team presenting their work to the whole business leadership. Here they received encouragement for all the work done. The work was affirmed or a suggestion was made to enhance it.

When the results were rolled out to lower levels there typically was one of great appreciation for the thoughtful work put forth. As small groups at the rollout affirmed the work, they were assuring one another that the work was good for the business and each of them. And they were given an opportunity to enhance the work presented, maybe the first time they had that opportunity. The whole workforce was beginning to unify.

The workforce was becoming teams of teams wherein the work could be done most effectively. Individually each member of the workforce is working where they are most effectively using their talent and experience.

Processes are documented everywhere within the operation from the leadership functions to the shop floor. All are owning and continuously improving their process, leading to operation excellence.

The whole workforce knows the destination, the mission and vision of the business. All are making decisions that are moving the business toward that destination. All are using strategies that work well together, are in unison. Progress toward the destination is known by all from the business leadership to the shop floor operations. It is a great state for a business to be in. The business management is evolving toward a Strategically Optimized Management System unique to that business.

My belief is that all who choose to use the 6-step process will have such an experience. Everything needed to guide leaders through the process is here in Part II–The Process, Chapters 4–9 including the appendices.

Put a stake in the ground. Commit the 2 hours a week to walk through the 6 steps. It will require thoughtful work over 2 hour meetings per week for many weeks. All work the rewards justify.

APPENDIX A
Glossary of Terms

Reference to the Glossary of Terms seeks to maintain a common language throughout the business workforce regarding the management system development and business operation. It is important that the whole workforce is using a common language.

CORE TEAM: A group of three to eight business leaders formed to develop a strategic plan, optimize the organization structure and match the right people to the right positions. A facilitator is needed to guide the process.

CURRENT SITUATION: A description of the current state of the business; How the current operation is performing as best surmised from the available data and the opinions of the staff, those being served, and other stakeholders of the business. It includes what is going well and what is not, encouraging, but brutally honest. It defines a starting point on which to build improvement. It may be useful to frame the current situation in terms of Strengths, Weaknesses, Opportunities and Threats (SWOT).

DESTINATION: Carrying out the mission and achieving the ideal vision of the operation is the business's destination to be pursued relentlessly.

FACILITATOR: One who will guide the members of a group through the Strategic Way Process referencing the 6 chapters of Part II and the 6 tasks of Appendix B.

FUNCTIONS: Activities that contribute to the production of the products and services of key result areas, tasks or processes.

KEY RESULT AREAS (KRAs): The major groups of functions assigned to specific areas that are key to the business achieving its mission and vision.

KRA OBJECTIVE/VISION: What is to be accomplished by each area through carrying out its functions. The KRA objectives and associated visions provide a clear target for each KRA and a means of measuring progress. Collectively met, the KRA objective/visions carry out the business mission and vision.

KRA STRATEGY: The approach selected from many that will best meet the KRA objectives when used to guide the business activity .design, staffing and operation. Collectively these strategies are a detailing of the business strategies.

KRA PROGRESS MEASURES: These provide data to evaluate progress toward the objectives/vision of each KRA as encouragement to leaders, staff and stakeholders and to guide process improvement.

LEADERS: Those who influence or guide the activities of a business, taking the people where they would otherwise not go.

MISSION: A business's highest level objective. All lower level organizational units such as departments, divisions, ministries, etc. use the term "objective" when referring to that which their unit is seeking to achieve to avoid confusion with the business's mission. Mission and purpose are synonymous, with mission preferred in today's culture. The mission answers three questions:

- What, in summary, is the work of the business?
- What is the object of the work or to whom is the work directed?
- Why the work is being done?

This expresses the overriding objective of the business, the reason the business exists and that which it seeks to accomplish.

OBJECTIVE STATEMENT: That which is intended to be accomplished by carrying out the activity or group of activities. Objective statements typically begin with, "To provide..."

RESOURCE GROUP: A group of people that are within or external to the business that are drawn upon by the Core Team to give specific insights when going through the steps of the Strategic Way Process™ .

STAKEHOLDERS: Those who have a stake in the outcome of the business's operation, e.g., workforce, users of the products and services, owners, suppliers, etc.

STRATEGY: Describes approaches selected from many that are intended to get to the business destination in the shortest possible time, with the least risk, most effectively using the minimum resources available.

VALUES: In strategic planning, identifies that which must be embraced by all members of the business to shape its existing culture in a way that the destination can be reached.

VISION: If the mission were being carried out ideally, the vision describes the ideal business operation activity and results one would see. Vision may be written from the perspective of those who have a stake in the mission. The vision statement adds great clarity to the mission. The mission and vision should be addressed together. A list of ideally expected outcomes may also add insight. The mission and vision clarify the intention of the business leaders, are inspiring yet constrain the business from taking on work that would dilute or defocus the leaders intended mission.

A glossary of terms (Appendix A) provides a common language associated with the Strategic Way Process and the Strategically Optimized Management System™ . For example, mission and purpose are typically viewed as synonymous in today's business culture. Mission is used here.

APPENDIX B
The Strategic Way 6 Step Tasks

"These tasks guide the facilitator in development of each
of the 6 steps."

Task to carry out Step 1

Develop a business level strategic plan

<u>Task Leader</u>: Business leader working with a skilled facilitator
<u>Objectives of the task:</u>
*   To provide a clear, concise long-term direction for the business
    expressed in a business level strategic plan format.
*   All who have a stake in the business have understanding and
    ownership in the plan and have the guidance to successfully
    implement and, when appropriate, enhance the plan over time.

<u>Outcome or Results of the task:</u>
*   A business level strategic plan is developed: An accurate
    description of the current situation, an appropriately scoped
    and inspiring mission and vision statement referred to as the
    destination, a committed set of values, a viable set of strategies
    to get to the destination and meaningful measures of progress
    along the way.

- The Core Team learns leadership and management concepts by effectively applying them as they complete the task.

Approach to carrying out the task:
- Form a Core Team of three to eight members (depending on the size of the business) made up of leaders of the business which may include some recognized as up-and-coming.
- The team meets twice (or a minimum of once) a week in two hour sessions. To meet less often than once a week results in loss of essential continuity of thought regarding the work of the task.
- A person skilled in facilitation is made available to provide guidance through the process with the Core Team members provide the strategic plan content. Two very different roles.
- Typically, the facilitator will guide brainstorming and consolidation to achieve desired results. For example:
  - Brainstorm strengths, weaknesses, opportunities & threats
  - Select the appropriate ideas and consolidate under the above categories. When the results accurately describe the current situation, move on to the mission statement, then to vision, etc. Weave in some history recounting the evolution of the business.
- The Core Team identifies a resource group to be called upon individually as needed to enrich the content of the strategic plan. This may include people within the business, suppliers, clients, consultants with specialized knowledge, repositories such as libraries and the Internet and the use of benchmarking. Over the implementation of the 6 steps of the Strategic Way Process™ , this group is normally 6-10 people but may reach 20 to 25 members.
- The Core Team develops a business level strategic plan guided by Chapter 4–Strategically Driven.

- Document the current situation using the SWOT process some history and current performance measures as appropriate.
- When the Core Team is satisfied that the description of the current situation is accurate and concise, declare a victory and move on to the mission statement
- Review and modify the current mission statement or create a new mission statement identifying the work of the business, the object of the work and why this work should be done.
  - To identify the work, the team may need to identify the business's categories of products and services, major transformations, core competencies, and thinking into the future as to what it could or should be.
  - Intertwined with the work, what is now, or could be the market for the products and services of the business.
  - Clarify the market at which the products and services are directed.
  - Considering the above while thinking through the work and the market, what is the benefit to the business? What is the benefit to the larger whole, that is, beyond the profit motive?
  - Encourage the Core Team to draft more than one mission statement, then analyze it, considering:
    - Is the scope of the work sufficiently broad or too broad? Do the same for the market.
    - Is it too altruistic, or not sufficiently so?
    - Is there a slogan or rallying cry that can be derived from the mission/vision? A number of years ago Xerox put a strong emphasis on functioning as a team internally and with customers with the slogan "Team Xerox." They put a banner bearing

this slogan across their high-rise office building. They were emphasizing an internal value and a marketing strategy. In just two words!

- When satisfied with the mission statement, declare a victory and move on to the vision statement
- Cast a vision of ideally carrying out the mission.
  - We will have succeeded if: lists the ideal or critical outcomes of carrying out the mission, a future state.
  - The vision narrative gives a word picture of what business operation looks like to ideally carry out the mission, often done with respect to the stakeholders in the business. Again, a future state.
  - Create a vision of ideal outcomes, critical to organizational development.
    - Describe the major outcomes of carrying out the mission as an ideal vision including the effect on the larger whole. For example, Henry Ford, George Eastman and Steve Jobs were thinking of products that would serve a market in which everyone, rich and poor, technically adept and not, could possess, make practical use of, and enjoy their products. For them, that was the benefit to the larger whole, the masses. At the same time, they grew large, profitable corporations.
  - When satisfied with the mission and vision statements, the business destination has been established. Declare a victory and move on to determine the values.
- Set values
  - That which the workforces as a whole values, however the culture evolved, may need to be enhanced to best ensure the mission and vision will be carried out.

- Thoughtfully consider what values must be culturally embraced to reach the business's destination
- Some existing values may need to be emphasized, some new ones introduced and some discouraged.
- The new or modified values will need to be modeled, emphasized and expected of all in the business.
- Ten values are way too many. One alone is missing an opportunity to shape the culture into a form that fosters reaching the destination while three make an effective target.
- After values are established the challenge is to think through the approaches, that is, the strategies that will lead from the current situation to the destination.
    - An effective way to start is to document the current strategies being used, although these are often not written down. That by itself is enlightening and doing so primes the pump to develop effective strategies.
    - When the Core Team has exhausted its insights, it is a good time to call in some of the Resource Group people. Share the current situation, mission and vision and ask them how to best move the business forward. Some other sources of input include literature and internet research, experts in the business's core functions, university types, etc.
    - Remember that strategy is always an evolving effort, revisited at least once a year, typically in June, with a 6-month separation from annual planning typically done in the November/December time-frame.
    - It is from strategies of the business's strategic plan that strategies are detailed out in the KRA's strategies. The business's strategies are the framework for the more detailed KRA strategies.

- Identify measures of progress to track movement toward the destination including:
  - Challenging the Core Team to identify the 8-12 measures that would accurately and comprehensively describe the performance of the business operation and progress toward the destination.
  - Lagging indicators are the bottom-line results that describe the performance of the business's operation related to progress toward its destination.
  - Leading indicators that predict from operations activity what the lagging indicator values will be.
  - Correlation of leading and lagging indicators comes with effort over time.
  - The fewer measures that accurately forecast the lagging indicators, the better.
  - The fewer measures that accurately and comprehensively describe the progress of the business's operation, the better.
  - Genius resides in the fewest measures used to forecast and describe progress. Redundant and less meaningful measures create confusion and add significant work to the operation.
  - Like strategy, measures of progress evolve with time. Establish a set of measures and expect to evolve them over time.

Responsibility and Authority related to this task:
- The sponsor assigns and funds the task and approves the results. The business's leader works with the facilitator to describe the task and take it to the sponsor for agreement.

- The leader reviews the task with the Core Team with the facilitator present. The leader is responsible for ensuring the task gets completed.
- The facilitator guides the process using Chapter 4, Strategically Driven, and this task strategy.
- The Core Team members provide the content for the strategic plan.
- The business's leader ensures that the Core Team and the facilitator keep their respective responsibilities separated.
- Toward the end of the strategic planning process, all members of the business are scheduled to be engaged through rollouts by the Core Team to communicate to the leadership and then to the whole workforce the work done to date, that is, the first draft of the business's strategic plan to:
  - Gain understanding and affirmation of what has been done and suggest enhancements.
  - Achieve ownership of this work and trust in the leadership of the business to have well-thought-out long range plans.
  - The suggested enhancements are reviewed by the Core Team to incorporate into the strategic plan as deemed appropriate. At the next rollout, the action taken on these suggested enhancements are fed back to rollout audiences. This accountability cements trust in the leadership. See Appendix C for the details of rollouts.

Accountability for carrying out this task: The business's leader, preferably accompanied by the facilitator, is accountable to the sponsor on an agreed-upon basis for the progress of this task.

Task Completion: The task is complete when the sponsor approves the business's strategic plan.

<u>Celebration when the task is complete</u>: Learn to recognize and celebrate victories. With the guidance of the business's leader, the sponsor provides an appropriate celebration event for the Core Team and others. Keep the event small, simple, and meaningful to those who contributed, use symbolism in keeping it inexpensive. Let victory celebrations become part of the DNA of the organization. See Chapter 16, Work Made Easier, for a more detailed explanation of celebrations.

<u>A typical meeting of the Core Team:</u>

Background: Imagine this fictitious company manufactures products and provides services for offices of any type. The Core Team consists of the CEO (Mike), the Operations Manager (Tim), Assembly Dept. Director (Ken), Human Resource Director (Gwen), Marketing and Sales Manager (Kathy), a highly regarded engineer (Jeff) and the facilitator (Steve). The Core Team has had a two-hour meeting once a week for several weeks. This team is currently in Step One–Strategically Driven of the Strategic Way Process™. The concept of this Core Team meeting dialogue is for the reader to get a sense of how these meetings are conducted. What follows is the typical dialogue at a weekly meeting.

Steve (Facilitator): Let's call the meeting to order. Looking in your three-ring notebook under Step One–Strategically Driven you will see that we have the Current Situation described in a draft on the first page. This is followed by our mission statement "Our Mission: "To provide a highly effective office system of machines integrated into software to support any business." Coupled with the mission is the outcome of carrying out the mission. We are now focused on describing the ideal vision of carrying out the mission. Let's begin with Mike. You agreed at last week's meeting to draft the ideal vision after we had a brainstorming session on this subject.

Mike: "From the outcome of the brainstorming session and with my thoughts about the business, I wrote the following (Mike reads his half page draft).

Steve: "What do you like about it? Mike, you might take notes about the comments that follow regarding your draft."

Tim: "I like the..."

Steve: Thank you. Others?"

Jeff: "I can resonate with..."

Steve: Thanks"

Kathy: I particularly liked..."

After the team seems to have shared "likes" Steve continues.

Steve: "Now please comment on how the draft could be enhanced"

Tim: "I think it would be valuable to add..."

Gwen: "I agree and I would add...

Kathy: "Another thing I would include...

After the teams seems to have offered their "enhancements" Steve continues.

Steve: Mike, would you use these comments to create a second draft of the ideal vision of the business operation for next week's meeting. At that time we will look at what the team likes about your second draft and provide you with enhancements to consider.

Steve: Our next topic on the agenda is a new subject in the task to carry out Step One to develop a business level strategic plan. (The facilitator has read Appendix B regarding the task to identify values that the workforce must embrace to shape the culture in a way that moves the business toward carrying out the mission and achieving the vision.) Now let's begin by brainstorming possible values to be considered.

Mike: "I would suggest..."

Tim: "How about..."

Gwen: "I would consider..."

Jeff: "I think it would be important to..."

Steve is thanking each for their ideas. When the group gets quiet Steve assigns a person to write a values draft for review by the team at next week's meeting.

In the two-hour session Steve may have time to introduce the subject of strategy development. This is done with the assigned authors writing drafts for the subject assigned to them. The authors take notes, write a draft from the notes and present the draft at the next meeting until the team agrees they have a draft they are ready to present at the next rollout to the workforce. In a two-hour session Steve, the facilitator, may have the team address three or four topics. This keeps the team effectively moving through the Strategic Way Process steps.

When the team gets through Step One business strategic plan development, Steve will guide the team through development of the Rollout presentation and the order of presentation to the workforce groups to which it will be presented. At the next meeting of the Core Team Steve will lead them through a processing of the reaction of the workforce to the rollout material. At this time the team will note the positive affirmations and incorporate some enhancements and discard others. The results of this processing by the team will be noted at the next rollout to assure the workforces that their insights were seriously considered.

In the weekly sessions that follow, the Core Team will continue to walk through each task identified in Appendix B to carry out the first three steps of the Strategic Way Process until these steps are completed.

Task to carry out Step 2

Optimize the business organization structure

<u>Task leadership, resources, responsibility, authority, accountability and celebration</u>: Same as task to develop a business level strategic plan.

<u>Task Objectives:</u>
*   To optimize a business structure that organizes major work functions for optimal effectiveness in reaching the destination by facilitating formation of the most synergistic functional relationships

<u>Outcomes:</u>
*   The organization structure reflects a logical grouping of work functions into KRA's.
*   Minimizes transactional use of resources
*   The Core Team, the leadership, and ultimately the whole workforce gain an understanding of the concepts of transformations, transactions, primary workflow and support to the primary workflow.

<u>Approach:</u>
*   Continue using the Core Team, resource group, etc.
*   The Core Team optimizes the organization structure guided by the narrative of Chapter 8–Structurally Optimized
    *   Give this step careful consideration as it is central to the rest of the Strategic Way Process steps
    *   Recall that form follows function
    *   Identify the primary business functions

- Group these functions into Key Results Areas (KRA's) considering:
  - Inter-relatedness, synergy, critical communications, overall effectiveness, etc.
  - Think outside the box of convention
  - Transformational versus transitional functions
  - Consider core competency issues
  - In house versus outsourcing
  - Research many free sources as well as utilizing internal R&D
  - Consider benchmarking
- Press to get the organization as flat as possible while still maintaining sound management of operations.
- Typically, three to eight KRA's are within the range to function effectively and continue to be well managed
- The KRA team leaders become the business management team
- Review the horizontal and vertical interconnectedness of the organization structure: The teams-of-teams concept.
- Typically do the next rollout when step three is completed– Career Matching: Begin immediately after the Business Level Strategic Plan is completed.

Task to carry out Step 3

Match careers to specific roles in the organization structure.

<u>Task leadership, resources, responsibility, authority, accountability and celebration</u>: Same as task to develop an business level strategic plan.

<u>Task Objective</u>: To build KRA team membership with people who can most effectively carry out the KRA functions while meeting their career objectives, making best use of their knowledge and skills

<u>Outcome or Results</u>:
*   The KRA team leaders are identified as becoming the Business Management Team (BMT). The current business leader is likely to be the team BMT leader, but not necessarily so. The BMT leader may or may not be a KRA team leader. The BMT leader may have sufficient responsibilities for representing the business as to have insufficient time to provide leadership to a KRA.
*   The BMT fills out the membership of each of the KRA teams ensuring that the human resources are allocated such that all KRA teams are able to successfully carry out their tasks.
*   The BMT assumes the role of the business's operations management.

<u>Approach</u>:
*   The Core Team guides the matching process using the Chapter 9–Career Matched process to select KRA leaders.

- The career objectives, strengths, past experience and education of the KRA team-leader candidates are clarified by having each candidate present a resume to the associates as a group. The group offers enhancements to the presenters.

- For a business to enjoy healthy, uncapped growth capability, the issue of how much value each individual adds toward fulfilling the mission and achieving the vision of the business must be continuously addressed. For the individual members' career plan well-being and value added is equally important.

- The leaders must seek those who can best add value for everyone's benefit.

- The knowledge and skills required to carry out the functions of the KRA leadership must be thoughtfully clarified. An open, transparent discussion needs to take place to assure that the knowledge and skills have been accurately identified.

- Leaders are assigned to each KRA position based upon the knowledge and skills needed by each team with an optimal match of those available. Ask one another thought-provoking questions during this assignment process as suggested in the narrative in Chapter 9.

- One or more team leaders may come from outside the business. A few may be left without assignments. The leaders and the sponsor need to commit to assisting in any way possible the placement of these people outside the business.

- The BMT, aided by the Core Team and the facilitator, assumes the role of filling out each of the KRA teams with the best match of knowledge and skills needed.

- Rollout to the whole organization providing highlights of only the business's strategic plan, presenting anew the optimized structure and the appointment of KRA team members to gain understanding, affirmation and ownership by the whole workforce. A brief description of the first three steps of the Strategic Way Process would be most enlightening and encouraging to the workforce. Briefly describe steps 4 through 6 yet to be carried out. See Appendix C, Rollouts, for details.
- Continue to use the Core Team, resource group, etc. for future business management system development.

Schedule: Begin immediately after the Structure Optimization process is completed.

Task to carry out Step 4

Develop KRA Strategic Plans

<u>Task Leader</u>: Each KRA leader working with a skilled facilitator

<u>Task resources accountability and celebration</u>: Same as task to develop a business level strategic plan.

<u>Responsibility and Authority related to this task:</u>

- The business leader works with the facilitator to describe the task and take it to the sponsor for agreement.
- The sponsor assigns the task to the business leader, funds the task and approves the results.
- The leader reviews the approved task with the Business Management Team (BMT) with the facilitator present. The leader is responsible for ensuring the task gets completed.
- The facilitator guides the process using Chapter 10, Strategically Implemented, and this task strategy.
- The KRA Team members provide the content for the strategic plan.
- The business's leader ensures that the Core Team and the facilitator keep their respective responsibilities separated.
- Toward the end of the strategic implementation process, all members of the business are scheduled to be engaged through rollouts by the Business Management Team to communicate to the leadership and then to the whole workforce the work done to date, that is, highlight the business strategic plan, the organization structure and career matching and in more detail the strategic plans at KRA level to:

- Gain understanding and affirmation of what has been done and suggest enhancements.
- Achieve ownership of this work and trust in the leadership of the KRA team leaders to have well-thought-out long range plans.
- The suggested enhancements are reviewed by the Business Management Team to incorporate into the strategic plans as deemed appropriate. At some appropriate time, the action taken on these suggested enhancements are fed back rollout audiences. This accountability continues to build trust in the leadership.

Task Objective:
- To provide a clear, concise direction for each KRA, to describe its destination and the path for getting there and the means to measure progress along the way.
- All who have a stake in each KRA have understanding of and ownership in the plan and have given the guidance to successfully implement it and enhance it over time.

Benefit: Each KRA and the KRA's collectively have the guidance to achieve the results needed for the business to carry out its mission and achieve its vision.

Outcome or Results:
- A strategic plan is developed for each KRA
- Each KRA team is learning leadership and management principles by effectively applying them.

Approach:
- Form a leadership team within each KRA.

- Each team will meet once a week for an hour to develop its KRA strategic plan
- Each team will identify people within and external to the KRA to be called upon as needed to enrich the content of its area strategic plan. This may include people within the business, suppliers, clients, consultants having specialized knowledge, repositories such as libraries and the Internet, and the use of benchmarking.
- An iterative cycle will take place between each KRA team and the Business Management Team (BMT) to assure the KRA strategic plans are consistent with and supporting of the business level plan. Collectively, the KRA plans must ensure that the business plan will be achieved. This critical test is the joint responsibility of the BMT and each KRA leader.
- Toward the end of the strategic planning process a draft of each KRA plan will be rolled out to the KRA members.
- With the strategic planning process completed, each KRA team will celebrate its success.

Schedule: Task completion, with critique and celebration

Resources: People, facilities, material, money, etc. available to do the task.

Responsibility and Authority:

Accountability: (When, where and how the team leader reports team progress and results to sponsor):

Task Completion: (Criteria for completion of task):

<u>Celebrate</u> (Leaders of KRA team provide an appropriate celebration event.):

Task to carry out Step 5

Develop the KRA team management structures for each area.

<u>Task Leader</u>: Each KRA leader working with the KRA team. It may be helpful to have a skilled facilitator guide the team through identification of the tasks within the team's area and through at least one task development.

<u>Objective</u>: Each KRA team is to develop the tasks and processes to carry out the functions assigned to that KRA.

<u>Outcome or Results:</u>
- Each KRA team will develop a minimum number of tasks to most effectively carry out the functions assigned in step 2, Structure Optimization.
- Each task will involve one or more step-by-step processes which break down the functions assigned to the task into doable processes.

<u>Approach:</u>
- Identify the minimum number of tasks required to carry out the functions assigned to the area
- For each task, develop a task agreement that includes task name, objective, desired outcomes, approaches (processes), resources, and schedules
- Within the KRA team, identify the leaders for each task.
  - Each task leader will then identify the processes used to carry out the tasks

- Each task leader will then identify the steps that will carry out the processes
- Replicate this approach for each task within the area. This may require an outside facilitator for the first task. The skill may now reside within the team for the remaining task and process descriptions.

Accountability:

- All task leaders are accountable to the KRA team of which they are a part.
- All process leaders are accountable to the task leader.
- The KRA team leaders will review their KRA task plans with the Business Management Team (BMT) for effectiveness and completeness

Task to carry out Step 6

Develop Performance Management System

<u>Task Sponsor</u>: Business Management Team (BMT)

<u>Task Leader</u>: Each KRA leader working with the KRA team.

<u>Task Objective</u>:
- To bring the work processes to excellence, fundamental to a healthy business.

<u>Benefit</u>: Each KRA and the KRA's collectively have the capacity to bring their processes to excellence, necessary for the business to carry out its mission and achieve its vision.

<u>Outcome or Results</u>:
- Processes evolve to excellence:
  - Processes are documented and followed
  - Processes are improved until they:
    - Generate consistent, predictable results
    - Achieve significantly better results
    - Produce excellent results
  - Each KRA team is learning the leadership and management principles of:
    - Continuous improvement
    - Performance management

<u>Approach</u>:
- Each task leader within a given KRA learns and practices the use of:

- The improvement cycle: performance analysis, improvement planning, improvement implementation and assessment of the effect of the implemented changes.
- Performance measurement, establishing correlated:
  - Lagging indicators of performance
  - Leading indicators of performance
- Objective matrices
- Conventional measures of performance; profit, unit cost, schedules met, units of production per time period, people attending an event, etc.
- Goals established and met:
- Cascading the goals down through the organization
- Planning and executing the planned gap closure
- Celebration of meeting goals

Schedule: Task completion, critique and celebration: As appropriate

Resources (People, facilities, material, money, etc. available to perform the task.): As allocated at the time of need

Responsibility and Authority:

Accountability (When, where and how the team leader accounts team progress and reports results to the sponsor): Process leaders are accountable to task leaders who are accountable to KRA leaders who are accountable to the BMT.

Task Completion: (Criteria for completion of task): Ongoing and updated as appropriate

Celebrate: Leaders provide appropriate celebration events.

APPENDIX C
The Strategic Way Rollout

When a team has completed work that needs to be understood, enhanced, owned, accepted by and complied with by a group of people, an effective process to accomplish this is a Strategic Way Rollout which will be referred to simply as a Rollout. A Rollout involves a brief presentation of the results of the team's work – the rollout, and the solicitation from the audience of what is liked about the work and suggestions for how the work can be enhanced.

For the rollout, the team needs to put their work in concise clear form to be presented in about twenty minutes. Keep the presentation simple in concept, not a lot of detail. The audience needs to first understand the big picture, an overview. Mark the presentation material as Draft. It needs to be easy to assimilate and open to enhancement. If the audience senses they may be given the opportunity to influence the plan they will feel ownership in it. Have members of the team present the material with the rest of team up front to demonstrate unity and commitment. Programing the presentation onto a screen or displaying it on a wall keeps the audience all focused on the slides as they are presented.

For the sake of simplicity, let us assume the audience consists of one hundred and fifty or less people. For larger organizations follow the concepts described below but for larger audiences. The great environment for getting a positive response from the audience is found in dividing them into small groups after the presentation. In these small groups each person is given a safe place with sufficient air time to express their views about the presentation team's work. Three members of each small group are given an assignment. One is to facilitate the small group agenda, another to act as scribe, that is, to cryptically document the group's comments and a third to use the scribed notes to report back their comments later when the small groups are reassembled into one large group again.

The facilitator's agenda in each small group is to ask their small group members to note what they like about the work presented. When the group has exhausted their insights into what they can affirm about the work, the facilitator will shift the focus to a second question. How can the work be enhanced? Again, the scribe will note the responses. The facilitator should always respond positively to an enhancement with a "thank you." Some in the small group discussion will say "white" and another will say "black". Smile and say thank you to both. The decision of whether to incorporate either will be made by the presenting team at a later date. Now is the time to foster participation not judgement. During this time the presenting team circulates among the groups answering any questions for clarity the small groups have and assuring that the group member's three designated roles are being carried out.

When the small groups have contributed all of their affirmations and enhancements, reassemble the small groups into one group again. The reporter from each small group will highlight one by one the likes and enhancements of their group to the reassembled audience using their scribe's notes. Give the reporters no more than three or four minutes to present to assure that it is highlights they are presenting and to allow time for every group to be heard. On a light note, threaten to hook them off the stage if they get to voluminous. Now the audience is hearing more about what is good about the team's work and witnessing a clear demonstration of the willingness of the team to consider suggested enhancements.

Two important responsibility have been given to the audience through these small groups: Acknowledge what is liked about the work, find where the work is lacking and offer solutions in the form of enhancements. No negative garbage dumping has been allowed, that is, just criticism of the work. When that occurs, the facilitators note that only likes or enhancements are being sought. Facilitators need to be firm about it.

Rollouts always reveal what resonates with the audience. This gives the presenting team confidence in the work they have done. It also makes a giant step in bringing unity within the audience regarding this work. *Ownership comes from understanding and from being given the opportunity to offer enhancements to the work*. And there are always some great ideas captured from the suggested enhancements. No matter how long the presenting team has worked on a task, the rollout typically produces some great enhancements.

With the opportunity to note what is liked and how it can be enhanced the audience is well on its way to acceptance of the team's work. *Even the most ardent naysayer will have to concede that the work of the team is worthy of consideration and some level of acceptance*. In the Rollout process the audience has gained a new dimension in the role of being a business team member. To legitimize a rollout, the team must promise to go back and consider every point in the feedback provided by the small groups. The audience must be assured that some though not necessarily all of the suggested enhancements will be incorporated in the final draft of the team's work. At some future date in some recognized way, the team must confirm that this has happened. This will be the wrap-up of the rollout.

A Rollout needs to be done in a series. A rollout to present the leaders at the highest level in the organization for which the presentation material is relevant. then to the next level down after consideration of the enhancements, then to the leaders at the next level down in the organization and so on to the floor-level workforce. This is a great opportunity to honor the leadership at the various levels.

The next opportunity to do a rollout is after the series of rollouts is complete for the strategic plan and when steps two and three of the Strategic Way Process are complete. This work will be of as much interest to the whole workforce as was the strategic plan. They will have experienced a Rollout and should be made aware that the organization optimization and matching process has been done. Those subjects will perk their interest! And it will demonstrate a clear commitment by the leadership to implement the strategic plan.

APPENDIX D

Insights toward more effective leadership

Servant Leader: Leaders must be sufficiently humble to seek and embrace help, and, acting as servants of the workforce, being open to making changes that may reflect on them personally.

Visionary / Manager team: Business's function best when there is an entrepreneur or visionary at the helm with an effective manager alongside leading the operation.

Resource void assessment: Where there is a lack of collective knowledge and experience in one or more key areas of the business, leadership must seek outside resources.

Long-range planning: A business rarely evolves in a clearly defined and effective direction unless there is deliberate effort to make this happen. In the planning process there is a building of unity and establishment of ownership of all the stakeholders.

Commitment to values: Of the many values that transcend an organization, identify those that need to be emphasized or introduced to create a culture that propels the business forward.

Long-range planning implementation: Implementation may well be blocked by a number of issues. Go through the five Strategic

Way Process implementation steps, steps 2 through 5, that remove common roadblocks, leading to a smooth running operation progressing toward the mission and vision of the business.

Regularly revisit the planning and implementation steps: A business is constantly evolving when new insights are being discovered. The mission, vision and values may not change for decades, but the strategies typically change ten to thirty percent annually.

All the elements of a strategic plan are necessary: Current situation, mission, vision, outcomes or KRAs, values, strategy and metrics are all essential to the successful implementation of a strategic plan. Leaving out any one of these elements of a strategic plan will limit the business's ability to successfully implement a long-range plan.

Strategic plan communications essential: Continuous communication of the strategic plan from top leaders down to the people on the floor is critical for successful implementation of a strategic plan.

Declare war on the status quo: Don't accept the business's current situation. Leverage your strengths as never before. Identify your weaknesses and turn them into needed strengths. Seize the opportunities that cross your path. Turn threats into advantages.

Learn and use Total Quality Management (TQM): The department head and the staff did not know the principles of TQM, yet with minimal guidance they applied them effectively. These and a host of other TQM principles are readily available today and should be sought out by the leadership and embraced at all levels of an organization.

Invest in continuous improvement: Allocate resources, especially time, to the improvement of the operation.

Leaders, humble yourselves: Be open to examination of your work, even if you believe it is presently being done successfully. Be ready to make changes, big or small. This will strengthen your influence above and below your level in the organization structure.

Lead by example: Leaders, lead by applying at your level that which you expect those at lower levels to adapt.

Leaders can and should foster team building and unity within their organizations, vertically and across all levels: If there is dysfunction in the leadership, going through the strategic planning process can build understanding and respect of each member by the rest of the team as a byproduct of creating a long-range plan for the business. Rolling out the plan throughout the workforce builds unity as will be seen as part of the Strategic Way Process™ .

Learn to listen to one another at and between all levels of the organization: In listening to one another we learn from one another, build mutual respect and trust, gain real friendships and increase the probability of gleaning what is most important to the business from the available resources. We were born with one mouth and two ears!

Career matched Leadership: Match people's career objectives, passion, talents, experience and formal education to the available positions.

A system of progress measures applied effectively is a powerful leadership tool: A well designed system of measures can bring unity to a group of people with a diverse set of knowledge and skills brought to bear on a target.

Goals and celebrations: Collectively setting meaningful goals against meaningful measures of progress, defining doable gap closure actions, tracking the progress and having symbolic, enjoyable celebrations, make up the recipe for successfully repeating the goal setting cycle over and over again.

Using the Strategic Way Process fosters the potential for transferring the operation to other sites: When the mission and vision are passionately held in the hearts of leadership that embraces the 6 steps of The Strategic Way Process™ , there is clear potential for creating a model of the organization's business, whether it be for profit or not-for-profit.

Need for a strategic plan: Every business needs a well thought out strategic plan that clearly communicates what is to be accomplished, a framework for how it will be accomplished, and means of measuring progress along the way.

Strategic Plan Communication: This long-range plan must be continuously communicated across the organization and not left gathering dust in leadership's desk drawers to die from lack of attention. All stakeholders must participate in its implementation.

CPSIA information can be obtained
at www.ICGtesting.com
Printed in the USA
FSHW020220021220
76377FS

9 781662 802317